THE PSYCHOLOGY OF ACHIEVING SPORTS EXCELLENCE

A SELF-HELP GUIDE FOR ALL ATHLETES

Larry M. Leith

Faculty of Physical Education and Health
University of Toronto

SPORT SBP BOOKS PUBLISHER

Library and Archives Canada Cataloguing in Publication

Leith, Larry M., 1949-
    The psychology of achieving sports excellence: a self-help guide for all athletes /
Larry M. Leith.

Includes bibliographical references and index.
ISBN 978-0-920905-13-5

    1. Sports--Psychological aspects. 2. Athletes--Psychology.
3. Success--Psychological aspects. I. Title.

GV711.5.L44 2008   796.01   C200-903091-2

Distribution worldwide by
Sport Books Publisher
278 Robert Street
Toronto, ON M5S 2K8
Canada

http://www.sportbookspub.com
E-mail: sbp@sportbookspub.com
Fax: 416-966-9022

Printed in China

ACKNOWLEDGMENTS

There are many people to thank for their contributions during the writing of this book. First, my wife Nancy, who always supports my projects and puts up with my spending long hours on the computer – thank you for your encouragement and ongoing support. I am also very grateful to the many students and athletes who have, over the years, asked the questions and offered the feedback that provided the focus for this book. I really appreciate the fact that you shared your experiences and asked such meaningful questions. I would also like to thank Jana Jansons and Masha Sidorova for their time and hard work in selecting the University of Toronto pictures that were used throughout this book. Both of you gave unselfishly, and your combined efforts made this a much better product. And last, but not least, I would like to express my sincere appreciation to the students who consented to have their pictures used in this text – you have made, and will continue to make, the University of Toronto proud to have such excellent athletes and special human beings.

PREFACE

Sport psychology is a relatively young field of study. In fact, in 1965, the International Society of Sport Psychology (ISSP) became the first professional organization devoted to the promotion of the discipline. Since that time, literally thousands of research studies, critical reviews, and meta-analyses have been published by sport psychologists around the world. This has resulted in a wealth of knowledge pertaining to the science of human behavior in the world of sports.

Unfortunately, as is normally the case in academia, this research has been made available only to other sport psychologists, as well as libraries in academic settings. I use the term "unfortunately" because this very valuable information is not easily accessible to the average person. In addition, since these publications are intended primarily for an academic audience, they are often written in psychological jargon that is difficult to interpret by anyone who does not have a degree in psychology. What is *really needed* is a book that translates this valuable knowledge into an applied and readable form that can be readily understood and implemented by anyone wishing to improve his or her sport performance.

The Psychology of Achieving Sports Excellence was written to address this important need. It utilizes all of the most recent research, but presents it in a user-friendly format that takes the mystery out of sport psychology. The concepts are clearly explained in *everyday language* that will allow the reader to take his or her sport performance to the next level. Case studies and notable examples from the world of sports are utilized to highlight the importance of the concepts being presented. In addition, every chapter provides checklists and measurement instruments that will help you develop a better understanding of yourself in the sporting environment. Of equal value, personal applications and self-assessments will challenge you

This book takes the mystery out of sport psychology.

to apply this important information to your own specific sporting situation. The mental preparation strategies that you will learn in this book will significantly improve your sport performance.

This book has primarily been written for the serious athlete who wants to take his or her performance to the next level. The concepts and suggestions offered throughout this text are equally applicable to recreational participants and Olympic or professional athletes. Any person who wants to improve his or her level of performance will benefit from the psychological tools and interventions provided in each chapter. As an added benefit, the information provided in this book will help you be a better teammate or fellow participant. It will give you a much greater understanding of how to provide the best possible support to your friends.

THIS BOOK WILL BENEFIT ATHLETES AT ALL LEVELS OF SKILL. PARENTS, COACHES, AND STUDENTS WILL ALSO FIND THE BOOK HELPFUL.

Other individuals will also find this book useful. Parents, for example, often find themselves in a "coaching" role. They are viewed as important role models for their children 24 hours a day, every day of the year. Children continually look to their parents for valuable advice. For this reason, a book of this nature is of significant value. Parents will greatly benefit from a better understanding of the psychological effects of sports participation. This book also provides them with hands-on applied knowledge that will ensure their children have a successful and enjoyable sporting experience.

Students who are taking formal courses in sport psychology will also find this book beneficial. Most standard textbooks are written in very theoretical language, with hundreds of individual research studies cited. Students often find it difficult to determine the most relevant pieces of information. To make matters worse, most classroom textbooks do not tell students how to *apply* the information provided. This book, on the other hand, was designed to provide only those concepts that have been clearly established over a large number of research studies. Of even greater significance, *The Psychology of Achieving Sports Excellence* tells you how to apply the information to your own particular sporting needs.

Coaches will also find this book to be a valuable supplemental coaching tool. In 2003, *The Psychology of Coaching Team Sports* was published to help coaches better understand the psychological aspects of performance. This book covers the same and even more topics, but explains the principles from an athlete's perspective. It therefore provides a valuable supplement to reinforce the coach's initial feedback. Finally, coaches can only benefit from developing a better understanding of sport psychology *through an athlete's eyes*.

In conclusion, *The Psychology of Achieving Sports Excellence* should be viewed as a worthwhile tool to help you on your road to improved performance. It is intended to provide you with a better understanding of how mental preparation strategies can improve your level of performance. Following the recommendations and strategies provided in the book will significantly improve your performance, but the book discusses only one tool for success. Remember, there is no substitute for good coaching, proper technique, and optimal conditioning. Sport psychology is often the deciding factor in sport, but only after these other conditions have been met. Also, the concepts outlined in this book *must be practiced*, just like your physical skills, before they become effective. So remember to build these mental preparation strategies into your yearly training program. This is most effective if your plan is developed in consultation with your coach.

How to Use This Book

The Psychology of Achieving Sports Excellence provides a relatively large amount of information. It is therefore important to remember that you don't necessarily need to start at the beginning and read each chapter in order. This applies regardless of whether you are an athlete, parent, coach, or student. Here are some brief suggestions for how each of the individuals just mentioned can best use this book.

Athletes who have reviewed the book report they have found it very effective when used like a recipe book. For example, if you are having trouble with nervousness, start by reading Chapter 4 and doing the self-assessment exercises and personal application sections. Then start practicing the interventions recommended, and you will soon experience lower competitive state anxiety. If you are having problems with your self-confidence, and all athletes do from time to time, then start by reading Chapter 2. It will help you better understand the concept and will give you some great suggestions for developing a higher self-confidence in your sporting abilities. Parents can use the book in exactly the same way. For example, once you have identified the nature of your child's concerns, just go to the corresponding chapter and work with your child to learn and practice the suggested interventions.

Coaches who are using *The Psychology of Coaching Team Sports* can first teach the mental training techniques in their usual order, then encourage the athlete to do his or her "homework" by reading the corresponding chapter in *The Psychology of Achieving Sports Excellence*. Once the athlete has completed the readings, self-assessments, and personal applications, a debriefing session between coach and athlete is highly recommended. That way, the coach can answer any questions the athlete has and ensure that the athlete has a

thorough grasp of the concepts. The coach can also provide feedback and offer suggestions regarding the athlete's personal application and self-assessment exercises. Finally, the coach will find the book a valuable supplement to reinforce what he or she has taught in practice.

Students who have reviewed the book, or sections of the book, report that it really *ties together* the material presented in traditional college or university textbooks. They also find it very beneficial to learn how to *apply* the sport psychology concepts. All students reported that they would use *The Psychology of Achieving Sports Excellence* to *summarize* the material provided in traditional sport psychology textbooks. Finally, all students expressed that is was fun to read the case studies and do the self-assessment exercises and personal applications.

CONTENTS

CHAPTER CONTENTS

CHAPTER 1

INTRODUCTION

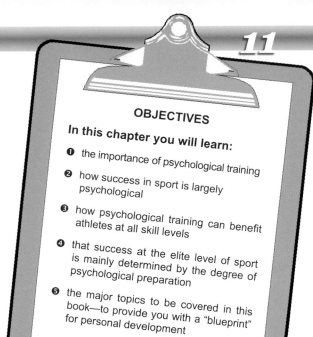

OBJECTIVES

In this chapter you will learn:

❶ the importance of psychological training

❷ how success in sport is largely psychological

❸ how psychological training can benefit athletes at all skill levels

❹ that success at the elite level of sport is mainly determined by the degree of psychological preparation

❺ the major topics to be covered in this book—to provide you with a "blueprint" for personal development

The scenario in the box below is by no means unique to the literally hundreds of thousands of athletes who aspire to take their games to the next level. An athlete, by very definition, always wants to get better and better relative to his or her opponents. Conventional wisdom has always suggested that the best way to do this is to practice harder and practice longer—not always a recipe for success! In some cases, this is

Randy is a tennis player who has been trying very hard to take his game to the next level of performance. He practices his technical skills regularly, does his aerobic roadwork, listens to his coach's suggestions, watches videos of the top performers in professional tennis, and thinks about tennis almost exclusively, but he still has not been able to advance in his club's rankings. Randy is starting to become frustrated in his quest to improve, but he does not believe he has the time, effort, and motivation to move forward. At this point in time, the options seem to be relatively obvious. Should he increase the intensity of his workouts even more, start a weight training regimen, seek out a new coach, practice longer hours, or simply resign himself to the fact that this is as good as he can be?

the exact prescription for improvement, especially if the athlete has not been putting out sufficient effort to elevate personal performance. But there are many more instances where the performer has "put everything on the table" but is still unable to see the much-needed improvements in performance to maintain daily motivation. What is that athlete supposed to do? Should he or she try harder, practice longer, or search out a new coach?

In this book, we will examine the issue exclusively from a somewhat different perspective—psychological training. In other words, what can you do from a psychological perspective that can take you to that next level of performance?

Can Psychology Really Make a Difference in My Sport Performance?

At the outset, it is important to recognize that success in any sport is the result of both physical and mental factors. Obviously, an athlete cannot advance to the next level if he or she has not attained an optimal level of physical fitness and technical expertise. To improve, you absolutely must "put in your time" in physical practice and skill learning. But remember, improving your sport performance is a relative concept—*it is contingent upon your present level of ability*. The young novice soccer player can benefit from this approach to the same extent as the varsity athlete or professional performer. This means that anyone can use sport psychology to take performance to the next level, regardless of starting skill level.

Most coaches and athletes will agree that success in sports is at least 40% psychological. Some researchers have even quoted figures as high as 80 to 90% in the literature. Numerous anecdotes from famous athletes support this. Some of the earliest examples include Roger Bannister, who became the first human being to break the four-minute mile. He has been quoted as saying that he mentally rehearsed the race repeatedly before the starting pistol commenced his race for fame. Similarly, a German bobsled team reported that they visualized their race more than 100 times before their Olympic event. More recently, Jack Nicklaus, arguably one of the best golfers of all time, has repeatedly pointed out the benefit of mental preparation in his sport. At one time, he was quoted as saying that success in golf is at least 90% mental. This is very strong testimony coming from a person who has won 18 major golf championships, currently 5 more than the present phenomenon Tiger Woods. Similarly, when Mark McGwire broke Babe Ruth's record for the most home runs in Major League Baseball history, he confided that one of the main ingredients of his success was isolating himself before each game and "seeing a mental picture" of the pitches that he would face from that day's starter.

Regardless of the exact numbers, the higher your skill level, the more important the psychological aspects of performance become. This means that a novice athlete can get better by utilizing the psychological principles outlined in this book. For example, a young figure skater can improve by visualizing his or her jumps and routine before a competition. Similarly, a young soccer player can get better at the penalty kick by "seeing" the shot before it is taken, just as a novice hockey player can improve performance by developing a "mental game plan" for the upcoming game.

At the other end of the continuum, professional and other world-class athletes can benefit tremendously from utilizing psychological strategies. When athletes get to this level of performance, there is very little to separate them in terms of technical skills and overall conditioning. It is therefore at this level that the greatest benefits of psychological training can be witnessed. At this point, the other factors associated with sport success are relatively consistent between athletes. For this reason, this book is devoted completely to teaching you the underlying strategies for mental preparation in sport. Once you have mastered these techniques, you will be well on your way to taking your performance to the next level.

Psychological practice is particularly important in sports where the number of repetitions is limited. Ski jumping, bobsledding, luge, pole vaulting, and diving all fall into this category of sports.

The Content of This Book

The content of this book is based on the research of the best sport psychologists from around the world. In each chapter, you will be briefly introduced to the most recent psychological theory, and then you will be given the opportunity to apply that theory to enhance your personal sport performance. In many cases, you will be provided with self-assessment exercises that will give you a better understanding of yourself and how you perceive your sporting experiences. Each of these elements will be important for your future success in sport.

Chapters 2 and 3 have been designed to help you develop the proper mental attitude for sport performance excellence. Chapter 2 presents you with a blueprint for developing self-confidence in your ability to succeed. It starts out by examining the differences between self-confidence, self-esteem, and self-efficacy, as well as their impact on your sport performance. The chapter then outlines the prerequisites for gaining and maintaining self-confidence in your present level of ability. Chapter 3 focuses on precompetition and competition mental-readying programs that will take you to the next level. In essence, this chapter provides information on motivation for peak performance.

Chapters 4 through 7 are directed more toward an understanding of the many factors in and around competitive sport that have the potential to hinder your overall effectiveness. These chapters provide you with a variety of mental preparation strategies for performance enhancement. Chapter 4 examines the relationship between arousal and performance. This chapter will teach you how to control your own levels of arousal and anxiety, thereby increasing your chances of ultimate success. How can you "get up" for the big competition without experiencing the anxiety that is so common in the sporting environment? Chapter 5 then follows with attention-control training strategies that will help you stay focused on task-relevant factors. In other words, how can you maintain your concentration at critical times in your sport? Chapter 6 exposes you to the topic of causal

Coaches must accept the challenge and responsibility for providing a good systematic training program that includes the physical, mental, and emotional components of training to maximize the performance potential of athletes.

attributions—the way you interpret success and failure and the effect those perceptions have on your subsequent motivation and performance. Chapter 7 concludes this section by examining the effect of the audience or spectators on your overall sport performance. In this section, you will learn how to "tune out" the spectators, or even "use" them for improving your skill level.

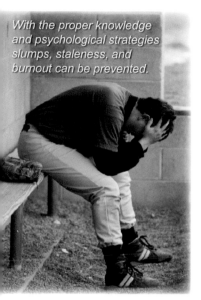

With the proper knowledge and psychological strategies slumps, staleness, and burnout can be prevented.

Chapters 8 and 9 look at potential problems athletes commonly experience, but ones that can be prevented with the proper knowledge and psychological strategies. Chapter 8 provides all the information you need in order to prevent slumps, staleness, and burnout. You will learn how to recognize the symptoms, how to prevent the problem from occurring in the first place, and in the worst case scenario, how to treat the problem effectively and get back on track in a short period of time. A normal competitive season is very long, and this prolonged exposure to the sporting environment can eventually take its toll on you if you are not careful. Chapter 9, the final chapter in this book, fittingly looks at the issue of ultimate retirement from your sport. You will learn whether or not there is life after sport when that dreaded day invariably arrives somewhere down the road. This chapter will provide you with the tools to ease this transition and be ready to accept and even enjoy new challenges.

In conclusion, it is gratifying to write a book that has so much potential to improve your overall sporting experience and skill level. By following the mental preparation strategies outlined in this book, you will be well on your way to taking your skill "to the next level."

KEY TERMS

psychological training   visualizing

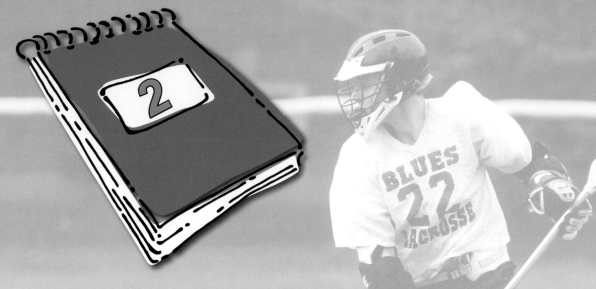

CHAPTER CONTENTS

CHAPTER 2

STRATEGIES FOR BUILDING AND MAINTAINING CONFIDENCE

OBJECTIVES

In this chapter you will learn:

❶ how to define self-confidence, optimism, and self-efficacy

❷ how to overcome some common misconceptions that can hinder the development of your self-confidence

❸ the tools to improve your self-confidence

❹ how positive self-talk can improve your sport performance

❺ guidelines to improve your self-talk

❻ how to overcome distorted thinking patterns that will hinder your sport performance

The scenario presented in the box below is by no means uncommon in the sporting environment. Almost every athlete has moments when he or she feels vulnerable to the whims of sport. What can an athlete do to build and maintain the optimum confidence to succeed? What

Wenda was having one of her best seasons as a varsity competitor in women's field hockey. Despite her success relative to previous years, she could not seem to shake the nagging feeling that this "high" was going to be short-lived. Before every contest, visions of performing poorly would play in her mind. In fact, the night before every competition would invariably see Wenda having trouble sleeping and imagining the worst of all possible sporting scenarios. This was becoming more troubling from week to week, leaving this excellent athlete to question whether or not she had what it takes to succeed in college sport. At this point in time, what she wanted most was simply to be able to feel good about herself as an athlete. She was completely tired of hearing the negative voices inside her head telling her she was going to perform poorly when it mattered the most. Wenda was willing to "trade her soul" for the ability to change all her negative thoughts to positive ones. But she did not know where to turn. . . .

was happening to Wenda, an exceptional athlete, that was causing her to doubt her athletic abilities? In this chapter, you will learn how to manage your thought patterns in a way that will put you on the path to maximum performance in your sport. You will learn how to recognize the internal enemies of self-confidence—and develop a workable plan to defeat them! Before starting on this journey, it is important that you clearly understand the exact meanings of the terms self-confidence, optimism, and self-efficacy. The following section will examine each of these issues and discuss how they affect your ability to see yourself as a seasoned athlete.

Understanding Self-Confidence, Optimism, and Self-Efficacy

The greatest athletes have high self-confidence.

When most experts try to define self-confidence, they mention terms such as "belief in one's powers" and "a state of assurance." Every great athlete (e.g., Michael Jordan, Tiger Woods, Jack Nicklaus, Roger Clemens, Wayne Gretzky, Muhammad Ali, Nadia Comaneci, Steve Nash, Mia Hamm, Lance Armstrong, Roger Federer, Edwin Moses, Serena Williams, Michelle Kwan) exudes this aura of self-assurance. Each of these athletes demonstrates an observable amount of self-confidence that could be viewed as a level of healthy arrogance. These individuals completely believe in their abilities . . . and it shows. A high level of self-confidence should be viewed as a good thing in competitive sport, since it often separates the good athletes from the great ones. By mastering the techniques outlined in this book, you will automatically increase your overall level of self-confidence.

Optimism represents a somewhat related concept necessary for the overall understanding of self-confidence. Optimism can be described as "the tendency to expect the best possible outcome in every situation," or "the ability to dwell on the most positive of all aspects of a situation." For example, an optimistic athlete who is

Mia Hamm

Learn to see opportunities, not problems.

facing an opponent with a superior record would tend to focus on the tremendous opportunity to "upset" the athlete who is viewed as more skilled, rather than imagining a humiliating defeat. This competitor would be straining at the bit to show the world what he or she can do. This ability to always look for the opportunity to shoot, score, or win, regardless of the odds, is a rare gift and is highly rewarded in athletics. So always remember to look at difficult situations as *opportunities*, not problems.

The last related concept is termed self-efficacy, which can be defined as a form of situation-specific self-confidence. This represents an athlete's tendency to believe in his or her ability to successfully execute a particular skill. You may find it helpful to think of self-efficacy as relating to specific techniques, skills, and even situations.

Self-efficacy is developed in four essential ways. First, you improve your self-efficacy through *successful performance*. This means it is very important for you to experience success for self-

A coach's verbal persuasion can be very helpful in developing your self-efficacy.

efficacy to develop. So make sure you set goals for yourself that are reasonable and within your reach, especially in the early stages of learning a new skill. Second, it is important to learn by means of *vicarious experience*. In learning new skills, every athlete needs a model or template to copy. So carefully watch your coach, a more-skilled teammate, or a video clip of a top-notch performer. Then, try to copy that effort in your next performance. Third, *verbal persuasion* can be very helpful in developing your self-efficacy. This usually comes in the form of encouragement from your parents, coach, or teammates. It is very important that each of these individuals focuses his or her comments on positive aspects of your performance. This will help you believe that you can succeed in your sporting efforts. Finally, remember that it is very important to maintain the proper level of *emotional* and *physiological arousal* to achieve top performance. You will learn all you need to know about this strategy in Chapter 4.

Taken together, self-confidence, optimism, and self-efficacy provide the recipe for your belief that "I can do this, and be successful, regardless of the situation." This feeling is absolutely crucial for attaining your ultimate success in competitive sport. In summary, always remember to keep an optimistic view in terms of your upcoming competition, and focus on developing the essential elements of self-efficacy. Rest assured that the results of your efforts will invariably lead to a higher overall level of self-confidence. You will be able to ride this combination all the way to the next level of competitive sport!

Common Misconceptions Athletes Have about Self-Confidence

Over the years, athletes have developed several misconceptions surrounding the issue of self-confidence in their chosen sports. Each of these faulty beliefs has the potential to undermine your ability to believe in yourself and therefore can impact your ability to ultimately succeed. Let's take a look at the most troubling misconceptions that have evolved and offer an alternative and more positive way of looking at each of these mistaken viewpoints.

Being Confident Is the Same as Being Arrogant

There is no doubt that certain amazing athletes develop a reputation for being somewhat arrogant. For example, Muhammad Ali, arguably the best heavyweight boxer of all time, was often viewed as having an overinflated ego. Deion Sanders developed the same type of reputation in professional football, as did Carl Lewis in track and field. Each of these individuals did indeed enjoy a somewhat "healthy opinion of himself." In fact, it was that exact quality that enabled each athlete to be the best he could possibly be. But it is not necessary to exhibit a similar loud and overwhelming self-confidence to be successful.

Michael Jordan

Confidence does not equal arrogance.

Consider athletes such as Joe Montana, the quarterback who led his team to four Super Bowl titles in the National Football League; Bjorn Borg, the winner of five successive Wimbledon titles in professional tennis; and Donovan Bailey, the 100-meter champion who set a world record of 9.84 seconds at the 1996 Olympic Games in Atlanta. All three of these athletes portrayed a quiet self-confidence and avoided the limelight during their exemplary careers. Regardless of your personal style, it is important to realize that you can be self-confident without being arrogant. Self-confidence is a learned behaviour. *And you absolutely need this self-confidence to be the best you can be in your chosen sport.*

Making Mistakes Will Destroy Your Confidence

One of the most important tasks for an athlete wanting to get to the next level is to get over the fear of failure. Human beings do invariably make mistakes, and you are no exception. Unfortunately, too many athletes respond to their mistakes with lessened self-confidence. If things don't turn out as planned, they feel less competent. This is most unfortunate, since making mistakes is a major part of learning how to get better. Athletes who continue to improve their skills gain self-confidence despite repeated failures or performances that were not up to expectations.

The significant thing that separates the athletes who learn from their mistakes from the ones who lose their self-confidence is the ability to selectively attend to and concentrate on each and every small improvement or positive experience. In fact, research verifies that this type of positive self-monitoring and focus is repeatedly associated with enhanced athletic performance. This highlights the fact that what happens to you in competition actually has very little to do with your overall self-confidence. *Confidence is more a result of how you think, what you focus on, and how you ultimately react to everyday experiences in your sporting environment.*

CONFIDENCE IS THE RESULT OF HOW YOU THINK.

Only Positive Comments Can Build Confidence

Learn how to turn negative comments into motivators.

Although it is important to receive positive feedback from your parents, coach, and teammates, it is also possible—and even desirable—to selectively perceive and reinterpret sarcasm, negative comments, and criticism in general as *stimulating challenges* and use them accordingly. For example, the coach or team member who criticizes your performance can be viewed as the ultimate motivator— the person who inspires you to prove him or her wrong! In the final analysis, this means that with the proper attitude and perspective, you can gain self-confidence even when you think you are being unjustly underestimated, overlooked, or criticized. *The bottom line is how you interpret and ultimately respond to negative comments.* Remember, "the only mistake that can happen is the one from which you fail to learn." Later in this chapter, you will be provided with the tools to make these apparent criticisms work to your advantage.

Success Always Builds Confidence

Maintain self-confidence to achieve maximum performance.

We have heard many times that "nothing succeeds like success," but this may not be completely true. Consider for example the star high school athlete who has just been accepted at a prestigious university or college. In a situation such as this, the real or perceived expectations run very high. This athlete is expected to succeed because he or she has succeeded before—bottom line. It is exactly this philosophy that makes the transition to the next level very difficult. This perceived pressure to continue to perform at the highest of levels invariably causes some athletes to lose their self-confidence, because their past success becomes an added source of pressure. *It is therefore very important that you do not limit your future success in sport because you lack the level of confidence your past accomplishments would suggest.* By working carefully with the concepts presented in this chapter, you will develop and maintain the self-confidence needed to achieve your maximum performance.

Either You Have Self-Confidence or You Don't

It is absolutely amazing how many athletes believe self-confidence is a trait that is genetic in origin. In other words, they mistakenly assume that self-confidence is something they are either born with or not, with no chance of developing it down the road. This viewpoint paints a very negative picture indeed, suggesting that self-confidence is completely beyond an athlete's control. In reality, nothing could be further from the truth! The high levels of self-confidence seen in exceptional athletes are by no means set at birth.

Self-confidence can be learned early.

A healthy level of confidence is the result of developing a consistent and constructive pattern of thinking that serves two very important functions. First, this technique allows you to remember and benefit from successful past experiences, focusing on all those things you did right in the competition. Second, it allows you to "let go of" or downplay past performances that were not up to your preconceived standards. *This means you gain self-confidence in the exact same way you learn other skills—by repetition and practice of the proper habits and techniques.* So make the commitment right now to follow the suggestions outlined in this chapter. If you do, you will see your self-confidence, and ultimately your performance levels, soar. The wise athlete who wishes to get to the next level will make this goal a top priority.

Strategies for Gaining Self-Confidence

Now that you know self-confidence is within your grasp, it is important to recognize the prerequisites for successfully developing that confidence. These underlying strategies include the following:

- Cultivating an honest self-awareness

- Understanding how thoughts and performance interact

- Embracing an attitude of sports excellence

- Developing an optimistic approach for explaining the "good, bad, and ugly" aspects of past performances

Let's look briefly at these strategies and see how each one can be put to work for you in your efforts to be the best you can possibly be. The following four suggestions will invariably help you develop and even maintain a healthy level of self-confidence in your sport.

Cultivate an Honest Self-Awareness

Learn how to win the battle with yourself.

Any attempt to gain control over your thoughts and feelings is an exercise that demands complete self-awareness. You need to be able to ask yourself, "Is my way of thinking *really* conducive to achieving sporting success?" And your answer must invariably be "Yes" if you are going to take your play to the next level. When you get right down to it, for most athletes, the toughest opponent is really the one who lies within, not another individual or team competitor. In other words, if you find that you frequently engage in self-criticism and experience feelings of hesitation and self-doubt, these occurrences are actually caused by faulty cognitive or mental processes, and they seriously affect your performance. What this really means is that to succeed in your sport, you need to learn how to win the "battle with yourself." This may sound easy, but it will be one of the most difficult struggles you will encounter on the road to athletic success. In this chapter, you will be provided with the tools that will allow you to win that battle, but remember, you must be brutally honest in your self-analysis regarding your thoughts and feelings.

Understand How Thoughts Interact with Athletic Performance

HOW WE THINK DETERMINES HOW WE FEEL.

A highly researched area in cognitive psychology called mood therapy suggests that *how we think actually determines how we feel!* With a few examples, you will have no trouble accepting this perspective. Think back to your own personal experiences in sport, and recall times when you told yourself that your opponent was too tough to beat, or that you were not prepared adequately for competition. What usually happened in the subsequent competition? If you practice the previous principle and cultivate honest self-awareness, you will probably say that you did not perform up to your normal standards. This is not at all unusual, because when you think negative thoughts, *you become anxious or nervous.*

Anxiety affects your performance in two very specific ways. First, anxiety results in increased muscle tension, causing the right muscles to be tense at the wrong time. Tense muscles invariably cause your coordination and timing to be seriously diminished. In competitive sports, this is a recipe for disaster. Second, the increased anxiety that results in a feeling of nervousness also affects your ability to focus on task-relevant factors in your sporting environment. Because you are anxious, you fail to "tune into" those elements of competition that are crucial for success. You also will find it more difficult to "tune out" those things that are distracting you from your ultimate goal of success. In this chapter, you will learn how to change the way you talk to yourself before and during competitions. In later chapters, you will develop the skills to manipulate your level of competitive anxiety and learn techniques for developing your maximum attentional focus.

Embrace an Attitude of Sports Excellence

In the last principle, you learned how your pattern of thinking can affect your overall sport performance. It is therefore important to develop a consistent and positive approach to viewing yourself in the best possible light. Here are a few tips that will help you develop an attitude of sports excellence—a "psychology of excellence" mentality that will take you to the next level of performance:

Remember to focus on your successes

This is not always easy, but it is very important to deliberately dwell on your day-to-day accomplishments, both in competitions and practices. You may find it helpful to keep a training diary. Record at least one example of performance success, one instance of great effort, and one example of personal improvement after each and every practice.

Remember to give yourself mental pats on the back.

Give yourself the same positive support you give your teammates

Over the years, you can probably recall numerous times when you offered positive comments and support to your fellow players. It is every bit as important to be as good of a friend and fan to yourself as you have been to your teammates. At the end of each day, make it a point to give yourself those "mental pats on the back" that you have so unselfishly offered to others on your team. This will help you view yourself in the most positive manner possible.

Be the artist of your own reality

It has been said that not one of us truly sees reality—we interpret what we see and call it reality! You can make this point work for you by interpreting day-to-day occurrences in a manner that increases your chances for future success. For example, if early in a contest you do not make that important free throw, penalty kick, or field goal, interpret this as a short-term setback that is preparing you for even better things later in the game. Tell yourself that you are still "working the kinks out" and can use this feedback to perform successfully later in the contest, when it really counts. On the other side of the coin, if everything goes very well early on, view this as a positive omen of how you will perform over the course of the competition.

Boldly pursue your dreams Every day, remember to tell yourself that "anything is possible," even if you have never accomplished a particular feat before. It is all a matter of believing in your abilities, being your own best friend, and constantly telling yourself that you can successfully go where you have never gone before.

SELF-CONFIDENCE PERSONIFIED

On August 20, 2006, Tiger Woods won the 88th PGA Championship at Medinah, Illinois, with an 18 under par 270 total. This victory was the 12th major championship won by Woods since his illustrious career began, second only to Jack Nicklaus, who finished with 18 majors. The story here is not that Woods won the tournament, but rather *how* he did it. He started the final round tied for the lead at 14 under par, and then he completely blew the tournament open with a round of 68 for the title. He did it as if no one else was even playing that day. Woods is 12–0 when leading or tied for the lead in a major championship. Pressure, it seems, is only a word to him. His amazing self-confidence is legendary, and it is this fact that sets him so far apart from the rest of the field.

Develop an Optimistic Approach for Explaining Past Performances

If you want to keep improving your sport performance, it is absolutely imperative that you view both your successful and unsuccessful performances in an honest and positive manner. Blaming the referee for a bad call does nothing to improve your next performance. Instead, focus exclusively on what exactly you could have done differently to achieve a more successful outcome. For example, after a loss tell yourself, "I could have come into the contest better prepared," or "I have to rethink my mental game plan." Chapter 6 provides you with the necessary tools to achieve this goal.

The Importance of Positive Self-Talk

By now you are certainly getting the message that how you talk to yourself is critical in terms of developing and maintaining your self-confidence—and your ultimate sporting success. You engage in self-talk any time you carry on an internal conversation with yourself. For example, recall times when you gave yourself instructions on how to perform a particular sport skill or skill segment, times when you encouraged yourself to try harder, and even times when you simply told yourself that you performed extremely well. These internal conversations can occur out loud, such as when you mumble to yourself. More often than not, however, they likely occur when you "hear these conversations" within your head.

The bottom line is that self-talk can become an important ally when it enhances your overall level of confidence, self-worth, and ultimate performance. It can help you stay focused on the task at hand and prevent you from dwelling on past mistakes or concerns. However, self-talk can become a liability if the internal dialogue is predominantly negative, a distraction to performing the task at hand, or so frequent that it hinders the automatic performance of your routine skills. Negative self-talk becomes a serious enemy when you evaluate a past performance and then engage in negative self-labeling, such as calling yourself a failure, loser, or even that dreaded term, "choker." Although it is important to rate your sport performance frequently and honestly, *there is absolutely no reason to label yourself, especially negatively*! Engaging in negative self-talk will not only affect your sport performance but also lower your overall level of self-confidence.

On the other hand, raising your self-confidence through positive self-talk requires a great deal of time and patience. You need to be continuously vigilant against the intrusion of unwanted negative thoughts or memories and the negative comments from so-called experts who set arbitrary limits on your sporting potential. You can fight back by focusing your mind on your present accomplishments

> POSITIVE SELF-TALK CAN IMPROVE YOUR CONFIDENCE AND PERFORMANCE.

and skill level, as well as developing a positive mental picture of your ultimate success. Always remember, *personal self-confidence both begins and ends in your own mind*, with self-talk playing the major role in determining whether your confidence level increases or decreases.

This section identifies the most common uses for self-talk in terms of elevating your sport performance. Research indicates that the following areas represent the most effective avenues for employing self-talk on your road to sporting success. These strategies will help you in your quest to do the following:

▶ Develop personal sport skills and achieve maximum performance

▶ Control personal effort

▶ Achieve and maintain the proper level of attentional focus required for success

▶ Create or change your emotion or mood

▶ Change personal bad habits

We will now examine each of these strategies and demonstrate how you can put the specific technique to work for you in your quest for peak performance. Remember, this will take time, just like learning a physical skill. You need to practice these suggestions on a daily basis, incorporating each into your yearly training schedule.

Self-Talk for Developing Skills and Elevating Personal Performance

Recent research shows that appropriate planned self-talk can significantly enhance your acquisition of sport skills. These findings also indicate that the overall pattern of self-talk you engage in will change as you become more proficient at your sport. For example, when you are first learning a new skill or skill segment, your self-talk

Self-talk is valuable for learning new skills and mastering old ones.

will be used primarily to remind you of the most important aspects of the particular movement or play pattern. Common examples include "Keep the left arm straight and take a slow backswing" in golf and "Keep the shooting elbow pointed toward the basket" in basketball. Keep the self-talk as brief as possible to ensure that you do not become more focused on the self-talk than you are on the performance of the sport skill. This can result in what is termed *"paralysis by analysis."*

As you master your skills, you will find that your self-talk will become shorter and will be needed less often. The focus of your self-talk should also shift from skill techniques to game strategies and positive feelings about the competition. Remember, the final goal is to reduce conscious effort, making the execution of the skill automatic. Self-talk is a means to get where you are going and is not to be seen as an end in itself.

Self-Talk For Controlling Your Overall Effort

Coaches can assist athletes in the development of verbal cues.

You can also use self-talk to help yourself maintain intensity and persistence toward your performance goals. For example, many athletes find it difficult to go to practice and put out maximum effort on a daily basis. If you can identify with these feelings, it would be wise to consider using self-talk to increase your motivation to practice. Internal dialogue such as "Just do it," "This is what it takes to become a winner," or "All great athletes pay the same price" can help you get out of bed and go to practice. Similarly, if you experience a temporary setback or competition loss, you can get yourself back on track by using self-statements such as "This loss just shows me that I need to work harder," or "Even Michael Jordan had an off game now and then." The key is to always focus on the positive aspects of your performance and recognize that any performance that is less than what you expected can likely be attributed to practice effort and intensity.

Self-Talk for Maintaining Attentional Focus

You can also use self-talk to control your focus of attention. Every athlete at every level of competition has experienced lapses in concentration, both during actual competition and in practice sessions. When this happens, it is wise to use personal verbal cues to keep your mind appropriately focused on the task at hand. In Chapter 5, you will learn a great deal more about attentional control, but the key here is to recognize that every athlete's attention is occasionally broken. For example, every striker in soccer will miss a penalty kick from time to time, and every volleyball player will miscue on a key set or spike over the course of a competition. But the successful performers find a way to put these negative occurrences out of their minds and quickly refocus on the next play. Self-talk such as "I'll make the next one" or "Now you really have my attention, so look out" will help you focus on the present and forget about the past. Remember, you can control only the present—never the past!

Self-talk helps you focus.

Self-Talk for Creating or Changing Your Mood

It is important to recognize that your mood can seriously affect your sport performance. In fact, mood can affect the overall pattern of your day, both in sport and in other areas as well. Can you recall a time when the alarm clock went off before you wanted to get out of bed, and you said something to the effect of "This is going to be a bad day"? And guess what—it probably was a bad day, wasn't it? That simple self-statement when you woke up set the course of negative expectations for the entire day. For this reason, many successful athletes wake up with self-statements such as "This is going be a great day," or "Today's competition is going to be my best yet." Remember, how you think and talk to yourself determines how you feel. And

Mood and performance are closely related.

research reveals that athletes perform better when they are in a good mood. So use your self-talk wisely to create a positive approach to both your day and your sporting activities.

Self-Talk for Changing Bad Habits

Every successful athlete finds it necessary from time to time to change a well-learned skill or habit because it is no longer working. This isn't always easy because you must unlearn a response that has become automatic and replace it with a new one. When you find yourself in the position where you must redirect a technique or game strategy, it is essential that you focus your self-talk on the desired outcome rather than on what you are trying not to do. For example, the hockey player who is misdirecting his or her slap shot because of the tendency to look up too soon should not use self-statements such as "Don't look up." Rather, he or she should focus on the positive, with internal dialogue such as "Keep your head down" or "One, two, look up" when completing the shot. Thinking about what not to do is a recipe for disaster, since it focuses your attention on the exact problem you are trying to correct. So always phrase your self-statements on the positive aspects of what you are trying to achieve.

Self-talk should focus on desired outcomes.

Common Distorted Thinking Patterns in Athletes

Now that we have looked at the importance of positive self-talk, we need to examine some of the most common negative thinking patterns that athletes typically use in their day-to-day routines. Table 2.1 summarizes these self-defeating statements.

Let's take a look at each of these patterns and see how each may be hindering your overall sport self-confidence. The first step in eliminating the negative elements of self-dialogue is to recognize their existence in the first place, so as you read through this section, ask yourself, in all honesty, if you have made similar self-statements in your sport of choice.

Table 2.1 Classification of common negative thoughts in sport.

1. All-or-nothing thinking	6. Magnification and minimization
2. Overgeneralization	7. Emotional reasoning
3. Mental filter	8. Using "should" statements
4. Disqualifying the positive	9. Labeling or mislabeling
5. Jumping to conclusions	10. Personalization

All-or-Nothing Thinking

TRY NOT TO VIEW EVENTS IN BLACK AND WHITE.

If you fall into this trap, you have a habit of seeing things in black-and-white categories. If your performance at any time falls short of your idea of perfect, you tend to see yourself as a total failure. For example, thinking that one single miscue in a performance, or one particular loss, makes you a lesser athlete is a common all-or-nothing categorization used by the majority of athletes. A self-statement such as "Since I missed that shot, I am not a good athlete" is absolutely self-defeating. It is imperative to recognize that no one is perfect, and you can never be perfect either.

Overgeneralization

Being late once does not necessarily represent a continual pattern of tardiness.

"Where is Simon?"

In this case, you see a single negative event as a never-ending pattern of defeat. If you have ever been late for a team meeting, you probably said something like this to yourself: "I'm always late for important appointments." Similarly, if you play basketball and miss a free throw, you may make the same mistake by saying, "I always miss free throws." Obviously, in reality, neither case is likely to be true —you were late *this time*, but you usually do arrive at the required time, and you can think of many times when you made important free throws.

Focus on what went right in your performance instead of what went wrong.

Mental Filter

If the mental filter is one of your problems, you are likely to pick out a single negative detail and dwell on it exclusively so that your vision of all reality becomes darkened, like the single drop of ink that discolors an entire beaker of water. For example, if you had a great overall performance on a given day, you may still have the tendency to focus on the one tiny aspect of your game that was less than perfect. This type of self-statement would probably be something like "It was a good game, but I showed my true form when I messed up that play." It would be far better to focus on *all of those things that you did well* instead.

Disqualifying the Positive

In this case, you have a tendency to reject or deny positive experiences or outcomes by telling yourself that they "just don't count" for some reason or other. In this manner, you can foster a negative belief in yourself that is contradicted by your day-to-day experiences. As an example, if someone compliments you on a great game, you may tell yourself, "It really wasn't that great of a game because I could have done better." If you have ever done this, your major problem is an inability to accept a compliment when it is given. People do not normally say nice things if they are not true, so learn how to take a compliment and feel good about yourself.

Jumping to Conclusions

Don't fall into the trap of mind reading.

This occurs when you interpret a situation negatively even though there is absolutely no reason to do so. As an athlete, you may tend to do this in two different ways. First, the "*mind reader error*" happens when, after a game, you may feel that someone is reacting negatively to you, and you just assume that the reason is your performance. You may tell yourself, "Mary is avoiding me because I did not meet

her expectations in today's game." It may very well be that Mary has something far more pressing on her mind at the moment, such as a problem at home, or maybe she is just not feeling well.

Second, the "*fortune teller error*" is a tendency to anticipate that things will turn out badly, and you convince yourself that your prediction is an established fact. Telling yourself "I am going to really screw up today" is an example of the fortune teller error. Face it, you cannot predict the future, so avoid these kinds of statements. Your self-confidence will be greatly enhanced if you anticipate the positive, not the negative!

Magnification and Minimization

This category is actually an extension of the mental filter distortion mentioned already. But in this case, it is even worse in that you exaggerate (magnify) mistakes while downplaying (minimizing) important aspects of your performance. If you have ever used a pair of binoculars, you will completely understand how this negative thinking pattern works. If you look at something through the binoculars the way they were intended for use, items in your vision appear much larger than they really are, but if you turn the binoculars around, those same items appear very small. Athletes have a tendency to view their efforts in the same way by saying such things as "That was a really bad shot I took, and we really needed it." This statement obviously represents the magnification error. Similarly, if you can remember times when you followed up the previous statement by telling yourself, "Those key shots just don't make up for my mistakes," you are guilty of the magnification/minimization syndrome.

Avoid the "binocular error."

Emotional Reasoning

If you have experienced this distortion, you have assumed that your negative emotions reflect the way things really are, such as "Since I feel depressed, sports must be depressing," or "I don't like the way that sports make me feel so nervous." Remember, what you feel represents only what you feel at that moment and in no way paints a picture of a gloomy sporting environment. And for your peace of mind, later in the book we will examine techniques that are far more effective to counter these feelings.

Using "Should" Statements

If you have a problem with this pitfall, you are the type of person who tries to motivate himself or herself with "should" and "shouldn't" statements, as if you have to be whipped and punished before you can succeed. For example, "I should do my roadwork, no matter how bad I feel today" and "I shouldn't miss a practice" represent this type of faulty reasoning. In both of these previous examples, the fact might be that you are coming down with a cold or the flu and just don't have the energy to perform your normal routine. Regardless, the only thing you can count on from the use of "should" statements is the feeling of guilt, anger, and resentment. You can quickly recognize that these do not make up a recipe for self-confidence.

Labeling or Mislabeling

DON'T LABEL YOURSELF BECAUSE OF A PAST PERFORMANCE.

This represents an extreme and ultimately damaging form of overgeneralization. Using a self-statement such as "Because I missed that important shot, I am an absolute loser" represents the labeling distortion. Or if a teammate made an important shot, you may tell yourself that "Billy is a star because he came through in the clutch." In either scenario, these were single, isolated sporting events that in no way reflect overall reality. Also, if you find yourself making self-statements that are emotionally charged or highly colored in language, you are likely defeating yourself with the mislabeling error.

Personalization

The last mental distortion occurs if you have ever found yourself uttering self-statements such as "We lost today because I had that bad argument with my dad," or "If I was a better person, our team would not have been eliminated from the tournament so soon." In both of these cases, you are seeing yourself as the cause of some external event that had absolutely nothing to do with you personally.

Let's take a few minutes to see which of these self-defeating thought patterns have been preventing you from achieving the self-confidence needed to succeed in your sport of choice. Go back through this section and identify when you have used similar internal dialogue in your past games or practices. Later in the chapter, you will learn how to change these thoughts into positive alternatives.

Personal Application 2.1 Identifying negative thoughts in your sport.

Take a few minutes to review the distorted thinking patterns outlined in this section, and honestly identify those categories and self-statements that may be hindering your sporting success. What are those self-statements? What category do they fall under?

_____

_____

_____

_____

_____

_____

_____

_____

_____

_____

_____

Techniques for Controlling Self-Talk Content

Completing the preceding self-assessment exercise is an important first step in the process of identifying the negative thinking patterns and self-statements that have been hindering your performance. But simply being aware of these thoughts is usually not enough. Once you have identified your negative thinking patterns, you need to learn how to start dealing with these thoughts. This process, known as **cognitive restructuring**, has been found to be the most effective technique for controlling self-talk. In this section, we will look at the two most important ingredients of cognitive restructuring: *thought stopping* and *changing negative thoughts to positive thoughts*.

Thought Stopping

If you find that your negative self-talk is frequent, consistent, and distracting, or if these thought patterns are creating self-doubt in your abilities, then it is imperative to eliminate this self-dialogue as it presently exists. One of the best ways to do this is a technique known as **thought stopping**. This process begins first with recognizing the unwanted thoughts, as done in the previous exercise. This will take a good amount of time, and you will need to go back over many previous practices and competitions to truly identify the most problematic self-statements.

The next step is to use a "trigger" to interrupt or stop the negative thought. The trigger can be a word or phrase, such as "Stop," "Stop these kinds of thoughts," "Red light," "Don't go there," or "Danger." Many athletes also find it helpful to visualize a stop sign, a red traffic signal, or a flashing road block. Other athletes prefer a physical action; try snapping your fingers or slapping your hand against your thigh. Maybe the best technique is to use one or more of these strategies in combination. But remember, thought stopping is a skill, and just like with any physical skill in your sport, you need to take the time to experiment with different strategies. This should be tried first in practice sessions, and then in actual competitions, but only after you have identified the particular strategy that works best for you personally.

Changing Negative Thoughts to Positive Thoughts

Learn how to turn negative thoughts into positive ones.

Although it is obviously very desirable to stop your negative thoughts altogether, this is not always possible, and it stops short of a better alternative. This better strategy involves learning how to replace any negative self-statements with positive ones that provide encouragement and bolster your overall sport self-confidence. As a simple example, if you find yourself experiencing an unwanted negative thought, such as "I'll never learn this play," try replacing this self-defeating thought with a better alternative, such as "This play is tough to learn, but I have learned new things many times before, and I can do it again." Learning how to change negative thoughts into positive ones is not an easy task, but it can be accomplished if you take the time to practice this skill.

Here are the main points you need to remember in acquiring this important skill:

Identify your own negative thoughts and develop a trigger to reverse them into positive ones.

▶ The first step is absolutely crucial. It requires you to identify the different types of negative thoughts that you have experienced, both in practice sessions and actual competitions. That was the purpose of Personal Application 2.1, so if you didn't do a thorough job of self-analysis, then go back and complete this task honestly and completely. It should take only a few minutes of your time to complete this task.

▶ The second step is to find a "trigger word" to initiate your thought-stopping procedure. You were provided with several examples of "thought stoppers," but remember that these triggers are completely personal, so feel free to substitute a word or phrase that works best for you.

▶ Practice replacing the original negative thought with a positive, self-enhancing statement—one that enhances your feelings of worth and self-confidence.

Table 2.2 gives examples of the most common distorted thinking patterns in athletes, offers possible thought-stopping techniques for your consideration, and provides you with sample positive thought replacements that are more self-enhancing for your future sport performance. These are examples only, and this information will work only if you personalize it to your own way of thinking.

Take a few moments to review the examples in Table 2.2, then proceed to the next self-assessment exercise. To complete the exercise, go back to Personal Application 2.1, expand your self-analysis if possible, record those negative self-statements that you identified, develop a thought-stopping strategy, and then replace your traditional negative thought with a positive one. This is the most important exercise of this chapter, so take the time to do it carefully—it will pay big dividends down the road.

For world-class race car drivers, a positive thought process is essential. A belief in their abilities, an expectation for the best possible outcomes, and the belief in themselves to successfully execute their skills and strategies are of the utmost importance.

Table 2.2 Examples of changing negative self-statements to positive self-statements.

Negative Self-Statement	Thought-Stopping Strategy	Positive Self-Statement
"Since I missed that shot, I am not a good athlete."	"Stop, that is just not true."	"I missed that shot, but I played great today."
"I always miss free throws."	"Don't go there."	"I make most free throws."
"It was a good game, but I showed my true form when I messed up that play."	Visualize a red stop sign, snap your fingers, and say, "No."	"My overall play kept us in the game all day, so one mistake is no big deal."
"It really wasn't that great of a game because I could have done better."	"Danger, danger, danger, not true."	"I need to focus on all of the things that I did well today."
"Mary is avoiding me because I did not meet her expectations in today's game."	"Forget it! How Mary feels is her problem."	"Mary must be having a really bad day today, so I should cut her some slack."
"I am going to really screw up today."	Slap your thigh and say, "That's ridiculous."	"I am going to have an absolutely great day!"
"That was a really bad shot I took, and we really needed it." "Those key shots just don't make up for my mistakes."	Visualize a road block sign and say, "Don't go there," or "No, no, no."	"Big deal, it was only one shot, so look out now." "Don't forget all the great plays you made today."
"I don't like the way that sports make me feel so nervous."	"Silly, silly me."	"Sports don't make me nervous, I do, and I can fix that with a better attitude."
"I should never miss a practice."	"Yeah, right, like no one ever misses a practice."	"I missed that one, but I will be at the next one."
"Because I missed that important shot, I am an absolute loser." "Billy is a star because he came through in the clutch."	"No, I am not a loser in any way." "That's rubbish, he misses shots too."	"I am a winner who just happened to miss one shot." "Billy is human, just like me."
"We lost today because I had that bad argument with my dad."	Visualize a slap on the wrist and say, "Dumb, dumb, dumb."	"We lost today because we weren't up to form, but we will nail them next time."

Personal Application 2.2 Replacing your negative thoughts with positive thoughts.

Negative Thought	Personal Thought-Stopping Strategy	Positive Replacement Thought

Summary and Conclusions

This chapter provides you with a better understanding of what is meant by the terms *self-confidence*, *optimism*, and *self-efficacy*. Self-confidence is a general feeling of self-assurance and a belief in your own abilities. Optimism is the tendency to expect the best possible outcomes from future sporting events. Self-efficacy refers to your belief that you can successfully execute any sport skill or strategy. These three ingredients, taken together, are highly predictive of your long-term sporting success. The chapter analyzes some common misconceptions about the whole idea of self-confidence in sport, then offers some important strategies for improving or enhancing your self-confidence as it relates to sport involvement.

The most crucial ingredient for building and maintaining personal self-confidence is *positive self-talk*. You learned the 10 most common distorted thinking patterns experienced by most athletes, discovered the necessary techniques for controlling your self-talk content patterns, and found out how to change your self-defeating negative thoughts into positive ones. Perhaps the most important outcome of this chapter is your identification in Personal Application 2.1 of the most frequent negative thoughts you experience related to your sport, and then your development of self-enhancing statements in Personal Application 2.2 to replace those negative thinking patterns. Once you have done this, you are well on your way to becoming a more confident and effective athlete. But remember, this mental skill needs to be learned and practiced, just like any physical skill. So get in the habit of making this a part of your yearly training program.

THE ATHLETE'S LIBRARY

Gould, D., Medberry, R., Damarjian, N., & Lauer, L. (1999). A survey of mental skills training knowledge, opinions, and practices of junior tennis coaches. *Journal of Applied Sport Psychology, 11,* 28-50.

Landin, D., & Hebert, E.P. (1999). The influence of self-talk on the performance of skilled female tennis players. *Journal of Applied Sport Psychology, 11,* 263-282.

Meyers, A.W., Whelan, J.P., & Murphy, S.M. (1998). Cognitive behavioural strategies in athletic performance enhancement. In M. Hersen & A.S. Belack (Eds.), *Handbook of behaviour modification* (pp. 53-65). New York: Plenum Press.

Rotella, R. (1996). *Golf is a game of confidence.* New York: Simon and Schuster.

Schunk, D.H. (1995). Self-efficacy, motivation and performance. *Journal of Applied Sport Psychology, 7,* 112-137.

KEY TERMS

cognitive restructuring   self-confidence   self-talk

mood therapy   self-efficacy   thought stopping

optimism

CHAPTER CONTENTS

CHAPTER 3

HOW TO "GET IN THE ZONE" AND ACHIEVE A PEAK PERFORMANCE

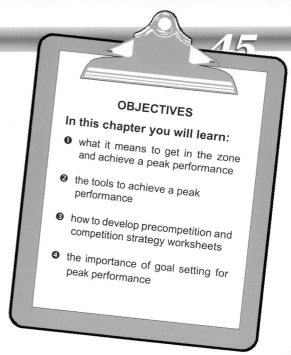

OBJECTIVES

In this chapter you will learn:

❶ what it means to get in the zone and achieve a peak performance

❷ the tools to achieve a peak performance

❸ how to develop precompetition and competition strategy worksheets

❹ the importance of goal setting for peak performance

The varsity athlete in the case scenario below was having quite a day. Every piece of the competitive puzzle seemed to fit together automatically to produce an outstanding sport performance. Almost every athlete has had moments like this at one time or another. Sometimes they last only a few minutes, and other times they last for the entire competition. But how can you explain such a surreal athletic experience? What psychological conditions are necessary to increase

Chris absolutely couldn't believe his luck. In this volleyball tournament, he was completely "on fire." Game after game and match after match, he continued to make all the crucial plays. More important, Chris knew with complete certainty that he was going to be successful in his bumps, sets, and spikes. This came as a completely unique experience, especially given the high level of competition. Even though this was one of the most important tournaments of the year, he surprisingly felt completely calm; one might even say "serene." When Chris was receiving serve, the ball seemed to just float toward him, giving him all the time in the world to set up properly to execute the perfect bump. Similarly, when he was on the attack, the ball from his setter appeared to be hanging on a string, just waiting for his devastating point-winning spike. Even before executing the plays, Chris somehow knew with an eerie certainty that he was going to make the big play. He could "see" each play happen, even before it actually began. It was like the world slowed down or ceased to exist. His actions felt as if they were occurring automatically. The only reality was the volleyball, and it became the center of his universe. In all his years of playing competitive volleyball, he could not remember one single day when everything had come together like it had today—he was truly in the zone.

You can increase your chances of achieving a peak performance.

the chances of experiencing an optimal athletic performance like the one just outlined? Are there any mental preparation strategies available that can increase your chances of achieving a peak performance? In this chapter, we will answer all these questions to your complete understanding and satisfaction. The information presented will go a long way in helping you "get in the zone," be the best you can be, and take your overall sport performance to the next level.

Defining Peak Performance and "the Zone"

PEAK PERFORMANCE IS AN ATHLETE'S DREAM COME TRUE.

The term peak performance refers to that magical moment when an athlete puts everything together—both physically and mentally. Our case scenario involving Chris paints an accurate picture of what that type of situation would look like if it happened to you. When this occurs, it results from a period of superior functioning, where you perform at a higher level than you ever have before. Athletes commonly refer to this as *flow*, or *being in the* zone. You have probably heard these terms before, but it is important to recognize that the ultimate experience for any athlete is to achieve a peak performance. A peak performance is an athlete's dream come true.

IN "THE ZONE"

On July 8, 2007, Roger Federer was crowned Wimbledon champion for the fifth consecutive year. He defeated Rafael Nadal 7-6 (9-7), 4-6, 7-6 (7-3), 2-6, 6-2 in the final of the men's singles. Federer equaled the record of Bjorn Borg, who won five straight Wimbledon titles from 1976 to 1980. Even more amazing, Federer's win marked his 55th consecutive grass-court victory, extending his Open-era record. Federer was "in the zone" when he won the title. He was quoted as saying, "I definitely had a period where it was so good, it was just incredible. . . . You're not afraid to try anything, you're not afraid to hit the ball hard, you're not afraid to go for aces. That's the sensation you get when you're playing so well. That's exactly how I felt today."

Unfortunately, the reality is that peak performances do not come along every day. In fact, interviews with hundreds of athletes suggest that they are relatively rare. In addition, many athletes intuitively believe that peak performances are nonvoluntary—they just happen. But is this really the case? Is it possible for you to be trained to experience more peak performances? Or at the very least, can you increase the chances of experiencing something closer to an *optimal level* of athletic performance? You will be happy to hear that research suggests certain psychological interventions can be implemented to increase your chances of a peak performance as well as the likelihood of getting in the zone and taking your game to the next level. In the remainder of this chapter, you will discover ways to optimize your personal performance. Feel free to call this flow or being in the zone, but the bottom line is that you will be performing at a higher level than you would normally expect. This is what athletic competition is all about!

You can learn how to achieve an optimal performance.

The Psychological Profile for Peak Performance

Before we even begin this section, it is important for you to realize that achieving a peak performance is the result of both mental and physical factors. In this book, we focus predominantly on the mental side of performance, but remember that you will never achieve a peak or **optimal performance** if you do not have the necessary level of physical conditioning, a complete knowledge of sport strategy, and a total mastery of the physical skills necessary for long-term participation. It is also important to recognize that a peak or optimal performance *is contingent upon each athlete's present level of ability*. This means young children starting their participation, skilled youth athletes at the next level, varsity performers, and even professional or elite international athletes can all experience these magical moments. The only necessary requirements are optimal skill and conditioning levels and a thorough understanding and application of the psychological interventions provided in this chapter.

Most athletes and even coaches acknowledge that success in sports

The better you get, the more important psychological factors become.

is at least 40% related to mental factors, perhaps even as high as 90%. In fact, the better you get at your sport, the more important psychological aspects become. This happens because athletes at a higher level of development or skill have already refined the strategies and physical skills necessary to achieve that level of performance. So for these individuals, psychological preparation becomes even more important, since it is the one feature that can separate the winner from the second-place finisher. For this reason, psychological skills training has become a crucial ingredient in most yearly training programs used by successful athletes. But before getting into a possible psychological skills training program for you personally, it is important to recognize that there is indeed an optimal psychological makeup for achieving peak performances. Several research studies have provided us with the information about psychological states most predictive of peak performance. This psychological profile is summarized in Table 3.1.

Table 3.1 The peak performance psychological profile.

- The feeling that performance is automatic and effortless
- The feeling of being in control—but not forcing it
- A high self-efficacy (situation-specific self-confidence)
- A positive preoccupation with sport—both imagery and thoughts
- An intense focus, with great concentration on the task at hand
- The feeling that time slows down
- A high degree of determination and commitment
- An energized yet relaxed feeling—an experience of no fear

The fact that these exact psychological mood states consistently precede or occur during a peak or optimal performance has led most researchers in the area of sport psychology to speculate that the right emotional climate, or conditions, can possibly set the stage for an optimal sporting effort. On the other hand, the flip side of this revelation is that a negative psychological climate—involving feelings of fear, worry, anger, and overall frustration—can have just the opposite effect, preventing you from achieving your best sport performance ever. For this reason, we now turn our attention to examining the best ways to foster the emotional climate to help you be the best you can be. The good news is that a consensus exists among experts in terms of which psychological skills can most effectively increase your chances of attaining a peak performance. The following section looks at the most popular mental training strategies for improving the quality of your performance.

Psychological Skills Necessary for Peak Performance

Several intensive research studies with athletes have investigated the mental preparation strategies and psychological skills that are used most often by successful elite athletes at every level of competition. Following is a brief summary of the common elements uncovered by this collective research:

THERE IS A BLUEPRINT FOR PEAK PERFORMANCE.

✓ Appropriate precompetition mental-readying plans

✓ Effective and well-developed competition plans

✓ Personalized and well-developed strategies for coping with distractions and unforeseen events

✓ Effective goal-setting strategies

✓ Effective use of imagery

✓ Proper arousal-management techniques—both energizing and relaxing

✓ Thought-control strategies for achieving proper attentional control

In the remainder of this chapter, we examine the first four of these strategies. Imagery, arousal-management techniques, and thought-control strategies are covered in subsequent chapters.

Developing Precompetition and Competition Strategies

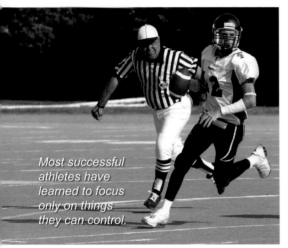

Most successful athletes have learned to focus only on things they can control.

There are many aspects of sport over which you have absolutely no control. For example, a questionable call by a referee, a bad bounce, a simple deflection, or an untimely injury can cost you an important victory. For as long as athletes have been competing in sport, uncontrollable situations such as these have always come along to let them down at an important moment. But the most successful athletes have learned that when preparing for a major competition, or any competition for that matter, *it is important to focus only on those things you can control.* As a serious student of sport, you have probably noticed that elite and world-class athletes tend to have a consistent approach to their pregame behaviors and performance. To produce consistent, high-quality performances each and every time they compete, it is necessary for them to develop a consistent set of psychological and behavioral routines that can be followed as a blueprint for success.

For this reason, elite athletes make extensive use of both precompetition and competition mental-readying plans. Once these plans have been developed and refined, they provide a consistent mental-readiness package to follow before competitions. But remember, just like any physical or technical skill, mental strategies must be practiced regularly to be effective tools in your quest for sports excellence. This is why it is absolutely imperative that you include these mental preparation strategies in your yearly training program. Over time, you will come to learn the particular mental strategies that work best for you personally.

You need to develop both a precompetition and a competition psychological plan.

Precompetition Mental-Readying Plans

The first type of mental training plan concerns itself with those specific thoughts and behaviors that occur from the night before your competition right up until the actual contest begins. Extensive interviews with athletes have determined the following most frequently mentioned aspects of a precompetition plan:

A precompetition plan is as important as the actual competition plan.

▶ Preparing and checking your equipment bag the night before a competition

▶ Using relaxation strategies the night before a competition, such as reading, taking a warm bath, or listening to your favorite music (Chapter 4)

▶ Making liberal use of imagery (visualization), where you "see" yourself performing successfully on game day (Chapter 4)

▶ Following specific wake-up procedures, such as time to set your alarm, your plans for breakfast, and the use of positive self-statements as discussed in Chapter 2

▶ Checking your equipment bag one last time, just to be sure

▶ Planning how you are going to travel to the competition site, allowing time for error

▶ Planning personal strategies for controlling your arousal level after arriving at the competition site (Chapter 4)

▶ Going through your pregame warm-up procedures

The main value of a precompetition mental-readying plan such as this is that it *helps you remove the "uncontrollables" from your precompetition routine.* Another very important feature of a precompetition plan is that it helps you focus on the upcoming competition while providing a workable strategy for creating and maintaining optimal activation and arousal levels that will lead to the best possible athletic performance.

Competition Mental-Readying Plans

The next type of mental training plan involves specific thought-content strategies for use during your actual competition. Following are the components of a competition plan for mental readiness most recommended by successful athletes:

▶ Personal techniques for focusing your concentration on task-relevant factors (the technical aspects of your performance)

▶ Developed strategies for dealing with pain and fatigue at critical moments

▶ Specific positive self-statements to maintain your confidence

▶ The use of cue words to maximize your performance

The general consensus is that approximately two-thirds of your total thought content during a competition should focus on task-relevant factors. Examples of task-relevant factors include statements such as "Knees bent and shoulder-width apart," "Keep your eye on the ball," "Stroke the tennis ball, don't hit it," and so on. These task-relevant factors are really just the many technical points you have learned from your coaches over years of practice. But it is exactly the use of this mental tactic that will help you stay focused on those skills and strategies that are necessary for an optimal performance. Because this strategy takes up a relatively large amount of all competition thought content, it will significantly reduce the chances that you will become distracted from the most important aspects of your performance. It will also reduce the chances that you will resort to anxiety-producing thoughts or concerns.

It is also very important to develop a specific plan for handling the pain and fatigue that will almost always occur during a practice or sporting contest. In Chapter 2, you learned about the importance of positive self-statements and how to use them properly. The same type of "mental pat on the back" has also been found to be highly effective in dealing with pain or exhaustion. For example, the track and field athlete who starts to "feel the burn" can benefit greatly by repeating positive self-statements such as "If I am feeling tired, my opponent is likely feeling worse, so keep pressing," or "Feeling tired is just another way of telling

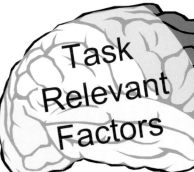

Task Relevant Factors

Two-thirds of your thought content should be on task-relevant factors.

Develop a strategy to deal with fatigue and pain.

me to work harder." To be totally effective, using self-statements in this fashion requires you to do the following:

▶ Be aware that you are going to experience fatigue and muscle pain.

▶ Recognize these feelings honestly when they occur, and don't try to deny them.

▶ Have a planned set of positive self-statements to get you through these times.

▶ Practice these techniques on a day-to-day basis, not just in the big game.

Positive self-statements are very important to help you maintain your self-confidence during a lengthy and tiring competition, so experiment with several to find out which ones work best for you personally.

One final set of self-statements deserves attention—cue words. Cue words can effectively improve an athlete's athletic performance, so you should give serious consideration to incorporating them in your competition plan. Cue words are words that have a specific personal, emotional, and highly charged connotation to them. For example, repeating words or phrases to yourself such as "Beautiful," "Great job," "Tremendous effort," or "Perfect" has been shown to result in improved self-confidence. The key point is that each and every athlete has certain words that can emit a favorable emotional response—that is, favorable in terms of improving practice or game performance. So it is very important to experiment with a variety of cue words to find the ones that are personally most effective.

Cue words will improve your sport performance.

Table 3.2 provides you with some examples of effective cue words that have been used by successful athletes, so start off by trying some of these in your next practice, and see if they work for you. The bottom line is that you need to develop *your own personal cue words* for each of the categories shown in the table. And remember, cue words do not necessarily need to make sense to anyone else, so be creative in your experimentation, then stick with those words that you find help you the most.

Table 3.2 Sample cue words that can improve your athletic performance.

Self-confidence: on plan, terrific, beautiful, great effort, superb, in the zone, perfect

Strength: crush, squash, break, destroy, annihilate, superman, topple, indestructible

Power: rip, explode, boom, drive, penetrate, thrust, kill, obliterate, smash

Speed: speeding bullet, lightning, fly, zoom, supersonic, dash, quick, zip, blast

Attentional focus: zone in, park it, block out, in the cocoon, lock in, grooved, intense

Persistence: in your face, crowd, worry, smother, stick, irritate, lock in, persevere

Remember, cue words must be highly personal to be effective. For this reason, it is a valuable exercise to start thinking about cue words you have used and found to be effective. It is also a good idea to develop a list of other cue words for experimentation in practice. Personal Application 3.1 will get you thinking in this direction.

Personal Application 3.1   Possible cue words that could work for me.

In this personal application, take a few minutes to develop some appropriate cue words that you think would work for you personally in each of the following categories.

Self-confidence: _____

Strength: _____

Power: _____

Speed: _____

Attentional focus: _____

Persistence: _____

Precompetition and Competition Strategy Worksheet

In developing precompetition and competition plans, most athletes favor the use of a specific worksheet, where behaviors and mental strategies are recorded for evaluation, revision, and future reference. Over time, these worksheets can be modified and refined to the point where they are ready for your implementation in important competitions. To get to this point, it is necessary to put a draft plan into practice in mock situations or low-key competitions. As mentioned earlier, these mental strategies must be practiced just like physical and technical skills to become effective for you as tools for success.

The worksheet you use can take on any form, although it should contain at least four specific dimensions:

▶ A description of the mental activity or behavior planned

▶ The desired effect you are hoping for from that particular strategy

▶ The result you actually get when you try that strategy

▶ A coping strategy (alternate plan) in case the planned strategy does not work in a practice session or in the actual competition

The concept of a coping strategy is especially important. Even with the best of plans, a particular technique or planned activity is not going to work perfectly every time. Similarly, one of those "uncontrollables" might just come along at the worst possible moment. For these reasons, it is absolutely essential for you to develop a coping strategy that can be substituted at a moment's notice. After all, a major competition is not the time to go back to the drawing board to design a new strategy. In addition, having a coping strategy already planned gives you one less thing to think about.

COPING STRATEGIES ARE AN ABSOLUTE NECESSITY IF YOU WANT TO PERFORM YOUR BEST.

Table 3.3 provides you with a sample mental preparation worksheet. Both precompetition and competition strategies are presented in one worksheet for your convenience. Please note that the coping strategy should be used only when the desired effect of the

Weather is something we cannot control. When presented with such a situation, it is essential to have a coping strategy that you can use at a moment's notice.

planned activity is not achieved. When this happens in practice or in a particular game, record this negative effect on your worksheet under the "Result" column (as shown in Table 3.3) right after the session. In the meantime, go with the coping strategy you planned as a backup.

Because all athletes will have completely different priorities concerning what they need to do before a competition, your worksheet may not look at all like a teammate's. Nevertheless, there is some value in comparing ideas with other team members in order to share strategies that seem to work or not work. And don't forget another valuable source of information—your coach. This individual has a unique perspective on what you need to do to get to the next level. For this reason, feel free to discuss your planned worksheets with your coach for possible feedback and modifications. But remember, the worksheet needs to ultimately reflect what you believe will work best in competition—it is highly personal.

Table 3.3 is designed to guide you in developing a precompetition and competition strategy worksheet (see Personal Application 3.2). But in the final analysis, your worksheet must be completely personal to effectively take you to the next level in your sport accomplishments. So take as much time as you need to start the preliminary planning for developing these mental preparation strategies.

Remember to try out each of these strategies in practice sessions. Then you can revise those elements that don't work and continue using the ones that do. It will take time to arrive at a final product ready for the big competitions, but your efforts now will get you started on a journey that will make you a much better athlete in the long run.

Now that you understand the key elements of precompetition and competition mental training plans and the importance of developing coping strategies, it is time to turn our attention to another important ingredient for achieving optimal or peak performance—goal setting.

Table 3.3 Precompetition and competition strategy worksheet example for a basketball player.

Activity	Desired Effect	Result	Coping Strategy
On the night before the big game, watch a good movie.	Feel no worries, relaxed, at ease.	Still tired, starting to worry.	Play a video game, listen to a relaxing CD.
On game day, sleep in; repeat positive self-statements such as "Today is my day."	Maintain relaxed feeling, feel fully awake, feel good, don't think too much about the game.		Stay in bed longer, think about your favorite summer vacation, listen to the radio.
Check equipment bag one last time.	Keep mind off big game, put mind at ease.	Still thinking about the game.	Read a novel, play cards with teammate, watch TV.
Spend 15-20 minutes alone to use positive imagery and rehearse your best moves.	Increase confidence, mentally practice defense strategies for key matchups.		If trouble concentrating, use relaxation techniques such as controlled breathing.
Travel to game site.	Arrive early to start preparations in a relaxed manner.	Car won't start.	Call a cab (use the number recorded on worksheet).
After arriving at game site, start some light stretches, do your drills, and go through your pregame shooting routine.	Feel loose, feel strong, no stiffness.		If trouble loosening up, do some light jogging, then run some shuttles before practice shots.
In the final minutes before tip-off, go off by yourself to mentally rehearse.	Concentrate on task-relevant factors, mentally review game strategy, eliminate negative thoughts.		If still worried or tense, perform either 5 to 1 count breathing or 3-part breathing to relax.
Mentally rehearse your first jump shot.	See your first shot as "nothing but net."		If having trouble, see your first bucket as a successful "give and go."
During the game, use positive self-statements such as "Way to go, Michael."	Maintain focus, stay confident, remain "in the zone."		If you start to lose focus, use thought stopping, then employ centering to regain attentional focus.
Employ cue words throughout contest.	Increase intensity, improve overall performance, play better.		Try some of your planned backup cue words.
Immediately after the basketball game, tell yourself "Great game," "Terrific effort."	Develop a positive expectancy for next game's performance, increase confidence, feel good.		If you think that was not your best game, visualize a previous great game and say, "Next time, I'll rock."

Personal Application 3.2 Your own precompetition and competition strategy worksheet

Precompetition Mental-Readying Strategies

Activity	Desired Effect	Result	Coping Strategy

Competition Mental-Readying Strategies

Activity	Desired Effect	Result	Coping Strategy

3

Goal Setting for Optimal and Peak Performances

Goal setting is essential for peak performances.

Over the years, a variety of psychological techniques have been identified as ways of helping athletes achieve personal growth and optimal sport performances. The use of goal setting is one of the most recommended methods for taking your performance to the next level. **Goal setting** is a specific aspect of motivational theory aimed at focusing your efforts and monitoring your overall progress and success. Successful elite athletes have been shown to engage in goal-setting strategies far more often than their less-skilled counterparts. But even more important, they *employ correct and established goal-setting guidelines*.

If you are wondering about the effectiveness of goal setting in improving your performance, a research study utilizing meta-analysis provides an excellent answer to this question. Meta-analysis is a statistical technique that analyzes the results of many research studies simultaneously to obtain a generalized and valid result. On the basis of 36 empirical studies, this technique concluded that goal setting results in significantly improved performances in both sport skills and other motor tasks. In addition, the study found that this improved performance is optimal when goals

- are set in observable and measurable terms,
- are made public,
- take into account both short-term and long-term objectives, and
- are set with specific participation from the coach and athlete.

In the following section, you will learn the goal-setting strategies that can make you a better athlete, both in practices and actual competitions. But before looking at specific goal-setting guidelines, it is important to examine the different types of goals that can occur within an athlete's sporting environment. A consensus exists among sport psychologists that it is useful to make specific distinctions between different *types* of goals.

GOALS MUST BE OBSERVABLE, MEASURABLE, AND ACHIEVABLE.

Subjective and Objective Goals

Goals that are unrelated to actual sport performance are called subjective goals. Examples of this type of goal are having fun, getting fit, meeting new friends, and feeling better about yourself. Objective goals, on the other hand, are specifically related to your sport performance. There are two different categories of objective goals—general objective goals and specific objective goals. General objective goals are more intangible, such as "cracking the starting lineup" or "being the best player on the squad." This type of goal provides you with a general direction of where you want to go but absolutely no specifics in terms of how to get there. Specific goals, on the other hand, outline exactly what behaviors you need to perform to improve your personal performance. Some common examples include improving your field-goal shooting percentage in basketball, increasing your on-base percentage in baseball, increasing your vertical jump in volleyball, or reducing the number of unforced errors you make in each tennis match.

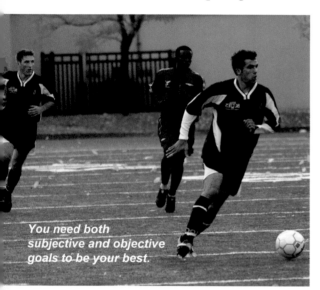

You need both subjective and objective goals to be your best.

Outcome, Performance, and Process Goals

Another distinction that has emerged from the sport psychology literature involves the relative value of outcome goals, performance goals, and process goals. Outcome goals refer to standards of performance that focus exclusively on the final result of a contest, such as winning or losing. Performance goals are different in that they focus completely on performance improvements over previous efforts, such as the number of points allowed per game in basketball, the number of yards rushing in football, the time in the 100-meter dash, or the successful height cleared in the high jump.

Finally, **process goals** are an extension of performance goals; they deal primarily with specific procedures you will perform during the contest. In golf, for example, the athlete focuses on keeping the left arm straight during the backswing and then keeping the head down during the follow-through. Other examples of process goals are any of the sample activities and strategies listed on the mental preparation worksheet in Table 3.3, as well as your Personal Application 3.2 exercise. Specific behaviors, points, and task-relevant strategies are required for your personal successful performances.

Successful athletes set three types of goals.

Goal-Setting Guidelines

NOT ALL TYPES OF GOALS ARE EQUALLY EFFECTIVE.

Now that you have learned that goal setting improves athletic performance, you need to realize that not all types of goals are equally effective in achieving positive results. Over the years, many excellent research studies in sport psychology have determined that certain types of goals produce better overall results. These guidelines are summarized in this section, so pay special attention to how you can start to use these goal-setting techniques to become the best athlete possible.

Set Specific Goals in Observable and Measurable Terms

Be specific in your goal setting.

A large volume of research in sport psychology, psychology, and organizational behavior has shown that to be effective, goals need to be expressed in explicit, specific, and, whenever possible, numerical terms. General or "do your best" goals have proven ineffective for improving performance. It is far better to state your goals in terms of observable and measurable behaviors.

For a goaltender in soccer, "Stop 6 of every 10 penalty kicks during our next practice" would represent a specific, observable, and measurable goal. Another example would be for a track athlete to say, "In my next speedwork session, I am going to run six 400-meter repetitions in 65 seconds or less." Both these examples are far more effective for improving performance than are general goals, such as "Be a better goalie," or "Run faster." These latter examples cannot be measured properly. Remember to use this goal-setting strategy religiously.

Set Positive Goals, Not Negative Goals

YOUR GOALS SHOULD BE STATED IN POSITIVE TERMS.

Any goal you set can be stated in either positive or negative terms. Research has shown that, whenever possible, it is best to focus on the positive behaviors that are required rather than on the negative behaviors that need to be eliminated. For example, it is more effective to have a stated goal such as "Increase my percentage of successful first serves" in tennis rather than a negative goal such as "Stop double-faulting so much." Although both goals are ultimately looking for the same result, stating the goal in positive terms will help you focus on success rather than failure. Sometimes just verbalizing a possible mistake to yourself can increase the chances of it happening, because unconsciously you are "seeing the error" before it happens. We will talk more about this concept in the next chapter.

3

Set Realistic yet Challenging Goals

Don't let your reach exceed your grasp.

Research has found a direct relationship between the difficulty of a goal and actual task performance. The more difficult the goal, the greater the chances for an improved performance. But keep in mind that this is true only when the difficulty of your goal does not exceed your actual ability to achieve that goal. In other words, you need to set performance goals that you are capable of accomplishing at your current skill level. Otherwise, unrealistic goals will invariably lead to frustration, failure, and eventually demotivation. So always remember to set personal goals that are difficult enough to challenge your ability but realistic enough to give you a chance of achieving that goal.

Set Short-Term as Well as Long-Term Goals

When most athletes are asked to describe their goals, they invariably identify long-range goals such as winning a scoring title, being MVP, making the all-star team, or making the starting lineup. However, research in sport psychology has discovered the need to set more immediate, or short-term, goals. One benefit of this approach is that it allows you to recognize your immediate improvements in performance. When this occurs, it increases your motivation toward achievement of the long-term goal you initially had in mind. You

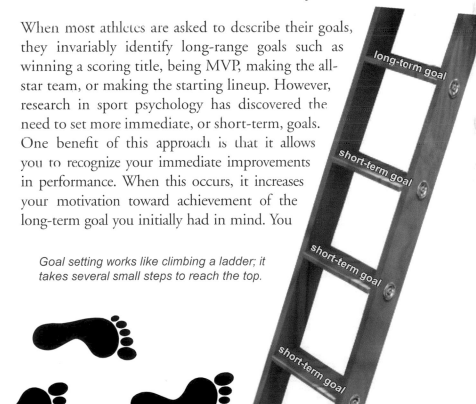

Goal setting works like climbing a ladder; it takes several small steps to reach the top.

could consider this technique a form of "building on success." Perhaps the best way for you to understand the relationship between short-term and long-term goals is to think of how a ladder works. It takes a series of small (short-term) steps to get to the top rung of the ladder. Goal setting for optimal performance works exactly the same way—you need to accomplish several small goals to reach your ultimate target.

Set Performance and Process Goals, Not Outcome Goals

Focus on what you personally can control.

When you observe the typical sports fan, that person can be seen to place tremendous importance on the outcome of sporting events. This is why society seems to identify so closely with sports heroes, revel in a team's victories, agonize over the defeats, or even start fights with fans from opposing teams. Unfortunately, outcome goals (focusing on either success or defeat) have been shown to be far less effective for athletes than performance goals. This focus on outcome goals has two inherent weaknesses. First of all, as an athlete, you have only partial control over the outcome of a contest. For example, if you play a team sport, even though you may perform at an all-time personal best, your team may still lose the game.

A second and equally important problem with outcome goals is that they will often distract you by creating a pervasive worry about the eventual outcome of the contest. When this happens, you lose focus on what needs to be done to perform at your best. A far better alternative is to focus on either performance goals, where you concentrate your efforts toward an actual improvement from a preceding contest, or process goals, where you devote your complete attention to the task-relevant strategies and procedures that will result in an excellent personal performance. So remember, set performance and process goals—and the outcome goals will eventually take care of themselves.

Set Practice Goals as Well as Competition Goals

Practice doesn't make perfect—perfect practice does.

In implementing a personal goal-setting program, many athletes make the mistake of setting goals that relate only to the actual competition or contest. While this is important in its own right, recent research suggests that elite, highly successful athletes also set explicit daily practice goals. Common examples of practice goals include "Remember to use cue words at times where maximum effort is required," "Make a minimum of 10 positive self-statements during each practice session," and "Concentrate completely on process goals today." When you learn to set practice goals, you will find that this technique increases your motivation to excel during the many hours spent in otherwise unexciting practice sessions. And once again, remember the ladder analogy—it takes many small steps to get to your destination at the top.

Personal Application 3.3 Setting personal goals for optimal performance.

Now that you know the goal-setting strategies most recommended by the experts, review this information carefully, then develop a series of personal goals that will start you "up the ladder" toward optimal performance.

I am going to implement these goal-setting strategies in the following ways:

➢ _____

➢ _____

➢ _____

➢ _____

➢ _____

➢ _____

Summary and Conclusions

A peak or optimal performance does not just happen by chance. In this chapter, you learned how achieving a peak performance, experiencing flow, or "getting in the zone" requires a series of well-developed plans that have the potential to elevate your skills to the next level. By now, you are aware that 40 to 90% of success in sports can be attributed to psychological factors. The higher the level of your skill, the greater the percentage that can be attributed to those mental factors. Developing a complete package of mental-readying strategies is not only desirable but also absolutely necessary if you want to achieve your full potential in sport.

The psychological skills that have most often been identified with optimal performance are the explicit use of precompetition and competition mental strategy worksheets, the use of coping strategies to overcome unforeseen events or incidents, and careful observation of the proper goal-setting strategies. Precompetition techniques help you focus your attention properly before the contest begins and take your mind off worrying thoughts that could distract your efforts. Competition strategies include concentration on task-relevant factors, methods of dealing with pain and fatigue at critical moments, and the use of cue words as a special type of self-statement. Finally, a series of goal-setting guidelines were provided for your careful consideration. If you follow the information and advice presented in this chapter, you will be well on your way to spending a good deal of your sport experiences "in the zone."

THE ATHLETE'S LIBRARY

Burton, D., Weinberg, R., Yukelson, D., & Weigland, D. (1998). The goal effectiveness paradox in sport: Examining the goal practices of collegiate athletes. *The Sport Psychologist, 12,* 404-418.

Eklund, R.C. (1996). Preparing to compete: A season-long investigation with collegiate wrestlers. *The Sport Psychologist, 10,* 111-131.

Filby, W.C., Maynard, I.W., & Graydon, J.D. (1999). The effect of multiple goal setting strategies on performance outcomes in training and competing. *Journal of Applied Sport Psychology, 11,* 230-246.

Kyllo, L.B., & Landers, D.M. (1995). Goal setting in sport and exercise: A research synthesis to resolve the controversy. *Journal of Sport and Exercise Psychology, 17,* 117-137.

Williams, J.M. (2001). *Applied sport psychology: Personal growth to peak performance* (4th ed.). Mountain View, CA: Mayfield.

KEY TERMS

competition plan

coping strategies

cue words

goal setting

objective goals

optimal performance

outcome goals

peak performance

performance goals

precompetition plan

process goals

subjective goals

zone

CHAPTER CONTENTS

CHAPTER 4

REGULATING YOUR AROUSAL AND ANXIETY FOR OPTIMAL PERFORMANCE

OBJECTIVES
In this chapter you will learn:

❶ to define what is meant by the term arousal

❷ about the relationship between your arousal and actual performance

❸ the optimal arousal level for your sport position

❹ to distinguish between stress and anxiety

❺ about the multidimensional nature of anxiety

❻ the difference between cognitive and somatic anxiety

❼ the tools to monitor your own anxiety

❽ interventions to adjust your level of arousal

As bad as it sounds, the situation below is not uncommon in competitive sport. It is quite common for an athlete to perform almost perfectly in practices, then have that performance drop off

Barbara was ecstatic when she saw the posted list of names announcing those athletes who had made the varsity squad for the coming season. Although she was entering only her first year of postsecondary education, she had been successful in demonstrating her remarkable talents during the grueling tryout sessions, and her coach had obviously noticed, placing her on the team. Although Barbara believed in herself, she was secretly pleased that she had been running the team plays so well in practice and that she had been "shooting the lights out" in her field-goal attempts. She was feeling pretty good about herself, all things considered. Unfortunately, however, in her first league game, things started to unravel. Her timing was repeatedly off when running set offensive plays, she was missing easy shots, and she felt indecisive in her efforts and decision making. What had come so automatically during tryouts and exhibition games was now feeling awkward and artificial. The situation continued to deteriorate, and Barbara was amazed to realize that she was not taking the easy shots when they presented themselves, but rather was passing off to a teammate. This trend continued both in practice and regular competitions for the next three weeks, leaving her coach no option but to bench her for another starter. Barbara just couldn't understand what had happened to her performance and why everything had turned upside down so quickly.

drastically once a formal competition gets under way. Ironically, the skills required in competition are exactly the same as those in practices, yet the results can be completely different. Why is it that an athlete can perform so well in one situation, then so poorly in another? What could possibly cause this performance drop-off, resulting in a dreaded "choke" when it counts the most? As an athlete, you will agree that this is as bad as it can possibly get.

In this chapter, we will look at the issue thoroughly from both research and practical perspectives. By the time you finish reading this chapter, you will have a workable understanding of this troubling phenomenon. You will also become familiar with the psychological interventions that can help remedy this type of problem and, more important, prevent it from happening in the first place. But before we do this, you must know exactly what is meant by the terms *arousal*, *stress*, and *anxiety*, as well as how they relate to your actual performance in sport. Surprisingly, over the years these terms have been used interchangeably and incorrectly. In fact, this same confusion has been demonstrated by athletes, coaches, sports writers, and even researchers. In the first few sections of this chapter, we outline exactly what is meant by these words that have caused so much confusion.

Understanding the Concept of Arousal

In the simplest of explanations, arousal can be viewed as a physiological intensity of behavior ranging from deep sleep to absolute frenzy. Arousal has also been referred to as activation, excitation, readiness, or drive. As an athlete, you already appreciate that a certain amount of arousal is required for an effective sport performance or effort. In physiological terms, arousal is defined as the degree of activation of the autonomic nervous system, or that system of organs and glands over which you have little or no voluntary control. For example, you do not have conscious control over your bodily functions of blood pressure, heart rate, or temperature. The autonomic nervous system is divided into two separate components—the sympathetic and the parasympathetic systems. The sympathetic system is involved predominantly with the bodily symptoms associated with arousal, such as sweaty palms, faster breathing, or increased heart rate. Over the years, many researchers have referred to this occurrence as the "fight or flight response." On the other hand, the parasympathetic system selectively reduces the effect of the sympathetic system. This brings your body back to a state of homeostatic balance, or where it should be—because the body "knows" it is unhealthy to increase arousal beyond a certain point.

The sympathetic system responds almost immediately to environmental happenings, or even an internal thought, whereas the parasympathetic system responds much more slowly in comparison. For example, a missed shot, a harsh word from your coach, or even an unwanted negative thought about a poor performance are all capable of causing an immediate sympathetic response. Conversely, your body could take hours to return to a nonaroused (relaxed) state after a negative experience during a contest. So although increased arousal can occur very quickly, getting back to an appropriate level will take more time than you can afford to spare in an athletic contest. The good news is that there are several intervention and stress-management strategies that can help you reverse the arousal response. The most effective of these tools are provided later in this chapter. The specific techniques have been time-tested by sport psychology researchers and, even more important, high-caliber and elite athletes. But before getting into this information, it is important for you to first recognize the actual relationship between arousal and athletic performance. This relationship has a profound effect on your behavior.

Competition causes activation of the autonomic nervous system.

The Arousal–Performance Relationship

Increased arousal improves performance to a point.

Over the years, a good deal of research has led to support of the inverted-U theory to explain the unique relationship between arousal and athletic performance. Stated simply, performance is improved by increasing arousal levels up to an optimal point, and then performance actually deteriorates with further increases in arousal. This relationship is illustrated in Figure 4.1.

This particular theory has led to the realization of two very important concepts for your personal consideration. Let's briefly discuss each of these principles.

Figure 4.1 The arousal–performance relationship.

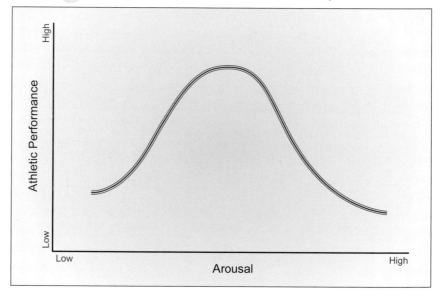

Different sport skills require different levels of arousal for optimal performance

Simple athletic tasks require a higher level of optimal arousal than do more complex tasks. A helpful way to understand this concept is to ask yourself the following question. If you were on national TV, watched by millions of viewers, and were

AS THE COMPLEXITY OF A SKILL INCREASES, THE AMOUNT OF OPTIMAL AROUSAL DECREASES.

offered one million dollars for the successful execution of a sport task, which of these skills would you prefer to attempt—making a basketball free throw or lifting a barbell equivalent to your weight completely off the floor to a standing position? Given that you had only one chance to execute the skill successfully, you would probably choose the weightlifting task. The heightened arousal resulting from the promise of mega money and being on TV would likely help your performance in the weightlifting, but it would invariably have the opposite effect with a fine motor skill such as the basketball free throw.

To summarize this relationship, as the complexity of a skill increases, the amount of arousal required for optimal performance of that skill decreases. Complex tasks are those involving precise movements, smaller and more numerous muscle groups, more external stimuli to deal with, and higher decision-making demands. Table 4.1 provides additional examples of this relationship.

Table 4.1 Optimal arousal levels required for various sport skills.

Sport Skill	Optimal Arousal Required
Weightlifting Sprinting Blocking in Football Shot put	Very High
Judo or wrestling Distance swimming or running Boxing	Somewhat High
Gymnastics events Soccer Basketball Field hockey, lacrosse Tennis, badminton	Medium
Baseball pitcher Baseball hitter Football quarterback	Somewhat Low
Shooting a free throw Kicking a field goal Putting in golf Serving in tennis	Very Low

It is important for you to consider where your particular sport fits on this table and how you can use that information to your advantage. The remainder of this chapter will help you in these deliberations.

Different skill levels require different levels of arousal for optimal performance

Athletes with different skill levels require different levels of arousal to perform at their best. For example, most athletes in youth sports will perform best with relatively low levels of arousal. These young participants have not yet reached the point where their skills are well learned and developed. For this reason, anything that increases arousal in novice athletes will likely distract their attention from the sport task at hand, thereby resulting in a performance drop-off.

Elite athletes require more optimal arousal to perform at their best.

Then, as skill level advances from novice through the various stages of competitive sport, including elite athletics such as varsity, international, semi-pro, and professional, relatively more arousal is needed to produce an optimal performance. These athletes have skills that are well learned and have been practiced almost to the point of being performed automatically. Once this happens, these top performers need more arousal to "get up" for the actual competition. This same principle explains why the most highly skilled athletes perform better in formal competitions than do their novice counterparts.

A major implication of this concept for your personal sporting success is that in the early stages of learning a new skill or sport strategy, you will need less arousal and should therefore reduce the number of external stimuli (such as friends or parents at practice) as much as possible. This same concept applies regardless of your level of skill development. Even professional athletes need to learn new plays with minimal distraction and relatively low arousal levels. So, if you need to learn a new skill, play, or strategy, it would be best for you to lower your overall level of anxiety. Later in this chapter, you will learn several techniques to manipulate your arousal to the point of being optimal.

MR. OCTOBER

New York Yankee slugger Reggie Jackson was nicknamed "Mr. October" for his clutch hitting heroics in the postseason, when it really counted. On September 14, 1977, while in a tight three-way race for the American League Eastern Division title, Jackson ended a game against the Boston Red Sox by hitting a home run off Reggie Cleveland. The Yankees won the division and then beat the Kansas City Royals to win the pennant. During the World Series against the Dodgers, Thurman Munson was being interviewed and suggested that Jackson might be a better interview subject because of his postseason success. "Go ask Mr. October," he said, giving Jackson a nickname that would stick. Jackson's crowning performance was his three home runs in Game 6, with each homer coming on the first pitch. With the fans chanting, "Reg-GIE! Reg-GIE! Reg-GIE!" the third home run came off Charlie Hough, a knuckleball pitcher, making the 475-foot blast one that stunned the ABC Television sportscasters covering the game. Howard Cosell blurted, "Oh, what a blow! What a way to top it off! Forget about who the Most Valuable Player is in the World Series. How this man has responded to pressure!" Jackson became the first player to win the World Series MVP award for two different teams. Mr. October obviously thrived in pressure-packed situations.

Determining the Optimal Arousal Level for Your Personal Sporting Success

Every athlete wants to know the "best" arousal level for every particular athletic situation. Unfortunately, because all athletes have different psychological makeups and tend to view sport situations from different perspectives, it is not possible to provide a simple answer to this question. For example, where one athlete might feel nervous because of an upcoming competition, another individual may see this same competition as an opportunity to demonstrate his or her skills and impress the coach. For this reason, you should instead ask yourself how your own personal optimal arousal level can be determined. Before you begin this process, realize that you must be completely honest with yourself. You need to recognize when you feel "up" and when you feel "uptight." There is nothing wrong with either of these emotions, but each can provide you with valuable information to improve your performance. The following exercise will get you started on the road to self-discovery in terms of personal arousal.

BE COMPLETELY HONEST IN YOUR SELF-DISCOVERY.

Using your honest responses to the questions in both parts of Personal Application 4.1, you and your coach can identify a variety of mental strategies that will change your arousal to the most appropriate levels at these critical times. Several of the most recommended strategies are outlined later in this chapter. In summary, the major goal of this exercise is to do the following:

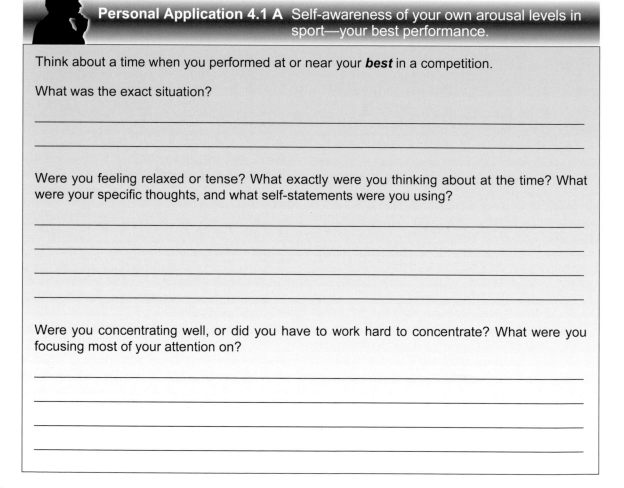

Personal Application 4.1 A Self-awareness of your own arousal levels in sport—your best performance.

Think about a time when you performed at or near your *best* in a competition.

What was the exact situation?

_____

_____

Were you feeling relaxed or tense? What exactly were you thinking about at the time? What were your specific thoughts, and what self-statements were you using?

_____

_____

_____

_____

Were you concentrating well, or did you have to work hard to concentrate? What were you focusing most of your attention on?

_____

_____

_____

_____

▶ Help you learn to identify your competitive feelings accurately

▶ Teach you to monitor your feelings and physiological responses during a sporting contest

▶ Remind you to focus on appropriate mental strategies that can improve your performance

▶ Help you develop the ability to control your thoughts and feelings to your advantage

Personal Application 4.1 B Self-awareness of your own arousal levels in sport—your worst performance.

Think about a time when you performed at or near your *worst* in a competition.

What was the exact situation?

_____

_____

Were you feeling relaxed or tense? What exactly were you thinking about at the time? What were your specific thoughts, and what self-statements were you using?

_____

_____

_____

_____

Were you concentrating well, or did you have to work hard to concentrate? What were you focusing most of your attention on?

_____

_____

_____

_____

The increased awareness that you gain from this self-assessment exercise will allow you to compare the feelings, thoughts, and emotions that accompany one of your best performances with those that accompany one of your poorer performances. By repeating this exercise over several sporting contests, you will be able to zero in on the exact arousal level that is most appropriate for optimal performance. It will also help you identify some of those self-defeating thoughts we discussed in Chapter 2.

Stress and Anxiety in Competitive Sport

In the previous sections, you learned that arousal refers to your level of activation or excitation. It is important to keep in mind that arousal in its most general sense is essentially neutral—it is neither good nor bad. All it really refers to is your degree of physiological readiness for action. Your most important goal, then, is to discover your own personal optimal arousal level for different situations. This chapter will help you do just that.

A somewhat related but more pressing problem is teaching you how to deal with the effects of stress and anxiety. At the beginning of this chapter, you learned that these terms have incorrectly been used interchangeably. We now turn our attention toward helping you distinguish between these two very important psychological issues.

Stress versus Anxiety

Stress and anxiety are not the same.

When we talk about stress, it is commonly defined by the experts as a nonspecific response of the body to any demand placed on it. Stress, just like arousal, can therefore be viewed as a neutral physiological response to something that is happening around you. Some types of stressors in life, such as winning a sports pool, winning an athletic award, or getting married, can be completely positive. In the psychological literature, this "good stress" is referred to as eustress. Of more concern to you as an athlete is the fact that some stressors you are exposed to can have a completely negative connotation. Examples of this include a trip to the dentist, a sports injury, or being told that your starting position is in jeopardy if you don't pick up your game. This "bad stress" is technically referred to as **distress**. Distress is typically manifested in the form of worry, tension, and anxiety. **Anxiety** is defined as the mental uneasiness you feel when you experience either fear or worry. Anxiety is a very complex psychological construct, and it is composed of several distinct elements. Let's take a few moments to consider the complicated nature of anxiety.

The Multidimensional Nature of Anxiety

The first distinction you need to consider is the difference between state and trait anxiety. **State anxiety** refers to a conscious feeling of worry or apprehension about a present or upcoming situation. The term *state* is used to indicate your immediate mood state, or "right now" kinds of feelings. State anxiety is fleeting, meaning it can vary a great deal over time. For example, before your first tryout begins, you will likely experience a great deal of state anxiety. But once the session gets started and you make your first basket, set up a key offensive play, or block a difficult pass, you will find that your original state anxiety quickly lessens or completely disappears. **Trait anxiety**, on the other hand, represents a relatively stable feeling or personality trait. For example, an athlete who is high in trait anxiety tends to be anxious or nervous across a wide variety of situations. Even worse, this anxiety persists over a long period of time. Athletes who are high in trait anxiety also tend to experience more state anxiety before upcoming contests than do participants with low trait anxiety.

Anxiety is a complex mental construct.

A second crucial distinction involves the components of somatic state anxiety and cognitive state anxiety. Somatic state anxiety refers to the physical component of state anxiety. You are experiencing somatic state anxiety when you feel muscle tension, faster breathing, sweaty palms, and an increased heart rate. Cognitive state anxiety is different in that it represents the mental side of state anxiety. During those times when you are fearing disapproval from your coach or teammates, worrying about losing a contest, or just failing in general, you are experiencing cognitive state anxiety.

How Different Types of Anxiety Affect Your Performance

The distinction between somatic and cognitive anxiety has allowed researchers to gain a better understanding of the relationship between precompetitive anxiety and your actual performance. As a serious athlete, these findings have special relevance for your future sporting efforts.

Cognitive anxiety is a major concern for competitive athletes.

ELIMINATE COGNITIVE
ANXIETY FOR
OPTIMAL SPORT
PERFORMANCE.

As a competition approaches, somatic and state anxieties affect your performance differently. For example, the increased sympathetic nervous system activity that you experience with somatic anxiety is natural and can be viewed as an indication of your readiness for competition. This somatic state anxiety will disappear shortly after your event begins. Conversely, the mental worry associated with cognitive anxiety represents a legitimate problem because it has the potential to cause a serious drop-off in your performance.

Research reveals that as somatic anxiety increases, your performance increases up to an optimal level. But once you get beyond this point, further increases in somatic anxiety will actually cause your performance to deteriorate. What this really means is that a certain amount of somatic anxiety is good for you, but too much has the opposite effect. Cognitive state anxiety, on the other hand, can be viewed as completely negative in its effect on your sport performance. Any increase at all in your cognitive anxiety will result in a less-effective competitive effort. This relationship can be better understood by viewing Figure 4.2.

Figure 4.2 Multidimensional relationship between athletic performance and state anxiety.

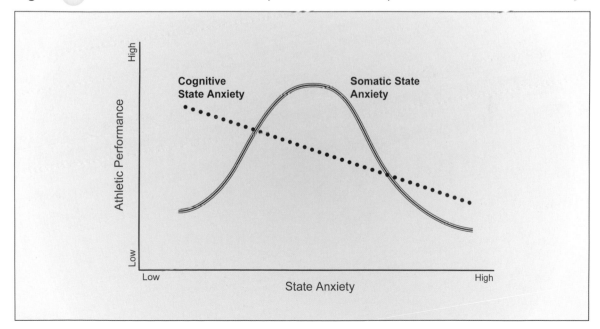

Since any amount of cognitive anxiety appears undesirable for optimal sport performance, you need to take steps to eliminate its occurrence. You may also need to use interventions if your somatic anxiety becomes too high. But before we examine the practical ways to control your somatic and cognitive anxiety, it is crucial that you learn to identify when these problems are actually occurring. This means we need to look at specific measurement tools for each of these anxiety types.

Measuring Your Personal Anxiety in Sport

Although the psychology and sport psychology literature can offer a wide variety of measurement techniques, there are two simple and easy-to-use measures that can give you a better understanding of what type of anxiety you are experiencing. The first one you can use by yourself, but the second should be used in consultation with your coach or a sport psychologist.

The Symptoms of Distress Checklist

It is crucial to monitor your own feelings of distress.

Earlier in this chapter, it was suggested that you need to identify and monitor your own feelings in the critical period leading up to, and including, the competition itself. In this way, you will learn the proper timing for using interventions that can bring your competitive anxiety back under control. One very valuable tool that will help you recognize the early indicators of state anxiety is the *Symptoms of Distress Checklist*. This checklist is provided in Table 4.2.

With this checklist, you simply mark any of the symptoms you are experiencing at any given time. With practice, this will allow you to recognize when state anxiety is approaching a problematic level that can hinder your performance. Once you recognize the problem, you can quickly implement the appropriate relaxation strategies presented later in this chapter to bring your anxiety under control.

Table 4.2 The Symptoms of Distress Checklist.

Cold, clammy hands	_____	Increased heart rate	_____
Cotton mouth	_____	Faster breathing	_____
Unable to concentrate	_____	Trembling hands	_____
Desire to urinate often	_____	Tense muscles	_____
Diarrhea	_____	Nausea	_____
Feeling of fatigue	_____	Voice distortion	_____

The Competitive State Anxiety Inventory-2

The best known and most often used paper-and-pencil test for state anxiety is the *Competitive State Anxiety Inventory-2* (CSAI-2). This instrument is designed to measure sport-specific cases of somatic and cognitive anxiety. It also measures your personal self-confidence because this dimension has been found to relate very closely with overall anxiety. Although the original test is composed of 27 statements, there is also a mini version that you will find easier and faster to answer. It will give you an equally valid assessment, and it is much more convenient for a competitive athlete to use. This test should be taken about 60 minutes before major, high-profile events. With competitive activities that are more recreational in nature, the test can be successfully completed about 15 minutes before game time.

But remember, you need to answer this inventory as openly and honestly as possible. If you "fudge" the answers, the test will be of absolutely no value in helping you get to the next level of your performance. Realize that certain amounts of nervousness and anxiety are completely natural and are experienced by all athletes at every level of performance.

Refrain from sharing your answers with teammates, since this will make it more tempting to answer the questions in a way that makes you look good. The only person you should consider sharing this information with is your coach, or a sport psychologist who is working with your coach to make you the best athlete possible. The CSAI-2 mini version is presented in Table 4.3.

Table 4.3 Competitive State Anxiety Inventory-2 (mini version).*

CSAI-2 (Mini Version)

Name: _____   Sex: M   F   Date: _____

Directions: A number of statements that athletes have used to describe their feelings before competition are given below. Read each statement and then circle the appropriate number to the right of the statement to indicate *how you feel right now*—at this moment. There are no right or wrong answers. Do *not* spend too much time on any one statement, but choose the answer that describes your feelings *right now*.

	Not At All	Somewhat	Moderately So	Very Much So
1. I am concerned about this competition.	1	2	3	4
2. I feel nervous.	1	2	3	4
3. I feel at ease.	1	2	3	4
4. I have self-doubts.	1	2	3	4
5. I am concerned that I may not do as well in this competition as I could.	1	2	3	4
6. My body feels tense.	1	2	3	4
7. I feel self-confident.	1	2	3	4
8. I am concerned about choking under pressure.	1	2	3	4
9. My heart is racing.	1	2	3	4
10. I'm confident about performing well.	1	2	3	4
11. I feel my stomach sinking.	1	2	3	4
12. I feel mentally relaxed.	1	2	3	4
13. I'm concerned that others will be disappointed with my performance.	1	2	3	4
14. My hands are clammy.	1	2	3	4
15. I'm confident about coming through under pressure.	1	2	3	4

* Adapted and modified from *Competitive anxiety in sport* by R. Martens, R.S. Vealey, and D. Burton, p. 177. Copyright 1990 by Human Kinetics. Reprinted by permission.

Scoring and Interpreting the CSAI-2

The CSAI-2 mini version is scored by calculating a separate total for each of the three subscales. Your score can range from a low of 5 to a high of 20 for each dimension. The higher the score, the greater your cognitive anxiety, somatic anxiety, or self-confidence.

To score the cognitive state anxiety subscale, total your responses for items 1, 4, 5, 8, and 13. Calculate your somatic state anxiety score by adding your responses for items 2, 6, 9, 11, and 14. Finally, totaling items 3, 7, 10, 12, and 15 will give you a measure of your self-confidence. In any subscale where you have chosen not to answer two or more questions, you should not use this measure because the information given was too limited.

Personal Application 4.2 Using the Symptoms of Distress Checklist and the CSAI-2.

Pick a time early in the season to try out the Symptoms of Distress Checklist. You might want to try this for the first time during an important practice or an exhibition game. Before that practice or exhibition game begins, mark the symptoms you are experiencing at that time. This will help you recognize when you are prone to arousal and anxiety issues. Once you have become comfortable with this tool, choose a preseason or exhibition game to answer the CSAI-2. It is a good idea to do this in conjunction with your coach or a sport psychologist so that the information can be shared afterward and appropriate interventions implemented.

Arousal Adjustment Interventions

Most athletes believe that if they train hard enough, practice regularly, and put out maximum effort, then everything should come together to produce a great performance. Unfortunately, experience indicates that this is just not true. Although your physical skills, overall conditioning, and game strategy remain relatively constant from one competition to the next, your actual performance level can fluctuate dramatically. Most sport psychology researchers believe that this variation in performance is caused by a corresponding fluctuation in your mental control.

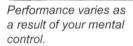

This concept of a fluctuation in mental control simply refers to the fact that you can, without knowing it, lose control of important cognitive functions, such as your ability to concentrate, your focus on the all-important task-relevant factors, and even your ability to process the relevant information in your competitive environment. In almost every case, this happens because you are experiencing inappropriate arousal or anxiety levels. The good news is that intervention strategies are available to help you manage these troublesome levels of arousal and anxiety, allowing you to get them under control *before* they can result in a poorer than expected performance. The remainder of this chapter focuses exclusively on highly effective interventions that can help you achieve—and then maintain—an optimal level of arousal. This will serve as a "safeguard" against the negative effects of cognitive anxiety and will ultimately produce a superior personal performance.

Performance varies as a result of your mental control.

Because athletes vary tremendously in their psychological makeups and experiences, it is important to realize that there will likely be times when you need to "psych up" before an event and other times when you need to "come down" in terms of pregame arousal. For this reason, we will examine specific intervention strategies for each of these scenarios.

Arousal-Energizing Strategies

SOMETIMES YOU NEED TO "PSYCH UP" FOR A CONTEST.

Most athletes and coaches refer to this type of intervention as "psyching-up" strategies. Regardless of which term you prefer, they both refer to techniques designed to increase your arousal level. Earlier in this chapter, you learned that too much arousal can hinder your performance. But it is equally important to recognize that too little arousal can also hurt your competitive efforts. You may remember times when this has happened to you. One of the most common examples occurs when you face a less-skilled opponent or an opponent you have beaten regularly in the past. Have you ever taken such an opponent too lightly? If you answered "Yes," then you likely had a less than stellar performance. Your arousal level was too low for you to perform at your best. Put another way, you just weren't "up" for the contest. To prevent this from happening again, you would be wise to experiment with one or more of the following arousal-intervention strategies.

Increase your breathing rhythm

One of the easiest techniques for increasing your arousal level is to simply focus on speeding up your breathing rhythm. First, concentrate on your regular, relaxed breathing rate. Take the time to experience how your breathing feels. Then, consciously increase your normal rhythm while imagining and feeling that more energy and activation are accompanying each successive breath. Some athletes have found it very helpful to use self-statements such as "Energy in" or "Charge up" with each inhalation and "Fatigue out" or "Temperature rising" with each exhalation.

Set situation-specific goals

In Chapter 3, you learned that goal setting can be a very effective way to prepare yourself for an important competition. In actual fact, most athletes will tell you they have little or no problem getting up for important contests or difficult opponents. But when interviewed more closely, these same athletes will admit they have experienced serious problems when facing a weaker opponent or a team they have beaten several times in a row. When this happens, you need to set personal performance goals for that particular opponent or competition. For example, if you are racing against inferior opponents in the 1,500 meters, set specific split times for each of the first three 400-meter segments of the race, and then if you meet these specific goals, you will be on course for an excellent final time. This is better than simply racing against less-skilled runners, any of whom could actually outsprint you at the end of the race. Another example is a tennis player facing an opponent whom he or she has beaten the last five matches. Two good situation-specific goals are to make 60% of your first serves and to commit only four unforced errors per set. The key to this strategy is that it will help you focus on a good performance rather than react to your less-skilled opponent. If you achieve your situation-specific goals, the end result will invariably be a successful outcome.

When facing an inferior opponent, set personal performance goals for that particular competition.

Use your personalized self-activation strategies and cue words

In the previous chapter, you learned the value of utilizing cue words to improve your performance. These same cue words can help you achieve your own personal level of activation and arousal. Over the years, elite athletes in almost every sport have used their own techniques to get psyched up for a big competition. Muhammad Ali used the mantra "Float like a butterfly, sting like a bee." This helped him reach his maximum level of arousal in his heavyweight bouts. It also served a dual function by focusing on task-relevant factors. Jimmy Connors, a past tennis great, used to slap his leg and repeat positive self-statements at critical times. This simple physical act coupled with internal dialogue helped Connors elevate his arousal and game to the next level. Similarly, football linemen often slap shoulders and butt heads to get up for a big play. But regardless of the sport or athlete, the common element suggests that you need to identify your own personal strategies to increase your arousal level as required. Since each strategy is completely individual, it is imperative that you experiment with several to find which ones work best for you, then practice them repeatedly throughout your yearly training program. That way, they will be ready for you when you are ready for them.

Personalize your cue words for optimal performance.

Try using visual aids to increase your arousal

Visual aids have also been found to be effective arousal energizers. Many athletes find it helpful to have a bulletin board in their rooms or dorms. This way, they are able to post notes or quotations that have an energizing effect. To be effective, these messages should always convey positive, self-motivating thoughts. Common examples include phrases such as "When the going gets tough, the tough get going," "When competing, don't get tense—keep a smile on your face, it makes more sense," or "Today, I will be invincible!" Coaches often use this same strategy by posting messages in the locker room such as "Every team must go through us to get to the championship." You will tend to remember these simple phrases and can draw on them when the competition intensifies. Another very effective visual aid involves reviewing videotapes of past successful performances.

Seeing yourself perform when you were at the top of your game can increase your confidence level and can also be very energizing before a major competition.

Arousal- and Anxiety-Reducing Strategies

You just learned several helpful tips that can elevate your arousal to an optimal level. But quite frankly, most athletes tend to have just the opposite problem and find themselves too aroused to be able to perform at their best. When you become overaroused, you are more likely to experience problems with cognitive anxiety—the type of state anxiety that causes your performance to deteriorate at critical times.

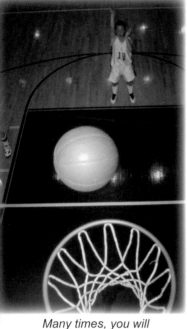

Many times, you will need to "calm down" to perform at your best.

One of the most terrifying words in the mind of any athlete is that dreaded term *choking*. You probably have your own idea of what this means, but the simplest way to view choking is *the inability to perform up to your previous standards*. This is caused by a combination of several factors, including overarousal, the loss of attentional focus, the perception of situations as being very stressful, the loss of personal control, and an underlying fear of failure. Each and every one of these factors will elevate your cognitive anxiety level and cause you to perform at a level that is much lower than usual. Cognitive anxiety might just be the most serious problem you will encounter in competitive sport. For this reason, the remainder of this chapter provides you with tools to cope with overarousal and keep cognitive anxiety from getting in the way of an optimal performance. Different athletes find different strategies to be more or less effective, so take the time to experiment with each of the interventions to find out which one or ones work best for you. It is always a good idea to try these out at home, during personal training, in practices, or during exhibition games. This way, you will have determined the best personal approach to arousal reduction before the big game starts.

Deep breathing One of the simplest tools to lessen your arousal level is **deep breathing**. This is why people are told to take a few deep breaths when they are becoming stressed out. You have probably seen this suggestion made many times. Also referred to as "the complete breath," this technique allows you to achieve relaxation through the use of proper breathing methods. Research demonstrates that taking a deep, slow, complete breath usually triggers a relaxation response. This intervention can be highly effective and can be performed in a very short period of time. The basketball player shooting a critical free throw will almost invariably use this strategy. Biathletes also use this method exclusively before squeezing the trigger in target shooting. You may even find it helps you fall asleep the night before a major competition.

Breathing exercises are very effective strategies for reducing arousal and anxiety.

Three-part breathing

A popular extension of deep breathing, three-part breathing is a very effective arousal-reducing strategy that combines controlled breathing with visualization (imagery). To perform this relaxation exercise, picture your lungs divided into three separate levels. As you start a deep breath, visualize the lower third of your lungs filling with air. As this happens, focus on pushing your diaphragm down and forcing your abdomen out. Remember to actually "see" the air level rising in your lungs. Continue this process by filling the middle section of your lungs as you expand your chest cavity and rib cage. Finally, visualize the top third of your lungs filling with air as you raise your chest and shoulders slightly. All three stages should proceed continuously and smoothly as you "watch" the air level rising in your lungs. Hold this deep breath for several seconds, then begin exhaling, this time visualizing the air leaving your lungs; first the top section, then the middle section, and finally the bottom third of your lungs. During this stage, pull your abdomen in (raising your diaphragm) and lower your shoulders and chest, squeezing the last air out of your lungs. Finally, concentrate on releasing all muscle tension at the end of the last exhalation. This will totally relax your abdomen and chest, causing an arousal-reducing effect.

5 to 1 count breathing

The 5 to 1 breathing technique requires you to first visualize and repeat the number 5 to yourself as you slowly take a deep, full breath. Exhale completely. Now mentally visualize and repeat the number 4 with your next complete inhalation. As you begin to exhale this breath, say to yourself, "I am more relaxed now than I was at number 5." *Focus on not rushing this thought.* Inhale once again while visualizing and counting the number 3. Then, while exhaling, say to yourself, "I am more relaxed now than I was at number 4." Allow yourself to recognize that you are feeling more relaxed. Continue with this process until you reach the number 1. As you exhale this last deep breath, tell yourself that you feel totally calm and relaxed.

This technique usually takes one to two minutes to complete. If you do it properly, it will always result in more relaxation than any single breath strategy. You may want to experiment with this intervention just before an important competition. Once you master this approach, you will be able to use it during actual competitions, given that you have suitable time.

Positive imagery The whole idea of imagery can be best understood as "seeing a moving picture in your mind's eye." Some people prefer to use the term *visualization*, but both terms refer to the same process. Positive imagery can be an effective intervention against cognitive state anxiety for two main reasons.

First of all, positive imagery will improve your sense of self-confidence and self-efficacy. For this to happen, you need to visualize yourself performing a variety of skills in your sport of choice. More important, these mental images must show you performing your tasks extremely well and ultimately successfully. You also need to focus on "seeing" and "feeling" yourself being very satisfied with your competition performance. The reason this works is that positive imagery improves your situation-specific self-confidence about an upcoming competition. The net result is a decrease in the amount of cognitive state anxiety you experience in your performance.

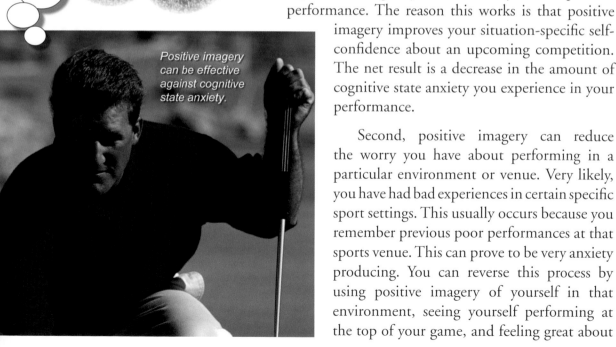

Positive imagery can be effective against cognitive state anxiety.

Second, positive imagery can reduce the worry you have about performing in a particular environment or venue. Very likely, you have had bad experiences in certain specific sport settings. This usually occurs because you remember previous poor performances at that sports venue. This can prove to be very anxiety producing. You can reverse this process by using positive imagery of yourself in that environment, seeing yourself performing at the top of your game, and feeling great about

IMAGERY MUST ALWAYS BE POSITIVE.

your accomplishments. Use this strategy repeatedly as the competition approaches. This mental picture of success will carry over, resulting in lower cognitive state anxiety. Your positive images have the potential to override the memory of previous past performances. Try using this technique every time before competing in the problem setting.

As a final hint, not every athlete is equally comfortable with using imagery. If you are having trouble visualizing, you may find it helpful to employ videotapes of yourself performing well at a different event. This will help you get the feel of "seeing yourself" perform well and will facilitate your ability to internalize—*and believe*—these mental pictures. And remember that positive imagery takes a great deal of practice, so use it religiously in your yearly training program. That way, it will be an effective strategy when you need it the most.

Mental Rehearsal

Mental rehearsal has the potential to improve sport performance.

Just like imagery, mental rehearsal involves "seeing a moving picture in your mind's eye." The major difference is that mental rehearsal involves visualization of a particular sport skill or skill segment. An impressive body of sport psychology research has demonstrated that mental rehearsal has the potential to improve your sport performance. Most of this research has been conducted on short-duration physical skills, such as delivering a particular pitch in baseball or cricket; shooting a free throw in basketball; hitting a forehand topspin in tennis; or "seeing" a particular dive, gymnastics element, or figure skating jump. It is important to realize, however, that this same intervention can be highly effective in longer-duration, more complex skills such as a set play in field hockey or ice hockey or a pinch in basketball. The main difference is that the mental rehearsal will take you a little longer with the more complex activities.

Mental rehearsal has been found to be effective for two distinct reasons. First, it completely prepares your mind and body for competition. Second, and more important, it is the most effective way to get you focused on task-relevant factors. This in itself will prevent the nagging and worrisome thoughts that create cognitive state anxiety. Although this sounds easy, remember that mental rehearsal is just like any other sport skill. It needs to be practiced regularly to be an effective tool in your quest to be the best you can be. For this reason, most elite athletes incorporate mental rehearsal into each and every practice session. It can be equally effective when performed off-site, such as mentally rehearsing a figure skating routine, a new team play, or a specific skill such as a backhand topspin in tennis or a penalty kick in soccer. To be successful, mental rehearsal must incorporate six specific features:

MENTAL REHEARSAL CAN TAKE YOU TO THE NEXT LEVEL.

► Whenever possible, your mental rehearsal should take place in the performance environment.

► It is imperative that you mentally rehearse the sport skill in its entirety, otherwise error points can occur (i.e., where there are mental breaks) that do not coincide with the actual rate you would perform that skill.

► The mental rehearsal *must* be seen as being performed successfully.

► A minimum of one mental rehearsal should precede a performance whenever possible, and events involving longer gaps in action require even more.

Mental rehearsal is a learned skill.

► Make sure your mental rehearsal approximates the actual rate of physically performing the skill.

► Try to concentrate on imagining the actual "feel" of the sport skill, just as you would with a physical skill.

In the final analysis, mental rehearsal does indeed affect your athletic performance. What you need to do is find the time and take the opportunity to use it. For example, if you are hitting an approach shot in golf, preparing for a free throw in basketball, or getting ready to attempt a first-service ace in tennis, you have ample time

You need to find the time and take the opportunity to use mental rehearsal.

Simulate what you expect in competition in your practices.

to perform several mental rehearsals before the act. In team sports, there is also plenty of time to use this strategy. In baseball, a relief pitcher can mentally rehearse his or her pitch selection for the next two or three hitters before being called into the game. A spiker in volleyball can "see" some perfect kills before being substituted into the match. And each member of a hockey shift can mentally rehearse a set offensive or defensive play before the puck is dropped. Mental rehearsal is once again effective in these latter examples because it will help you prepare for action and focus on the all-important task-relevant factors. It has the added bonus of reducing your cognitive state anxiety before the actual play unfolds.

Simulations

Another arousal- and anxiety-reducing intervention is the use of simulations. Simulation involves creating conditions in your practice sessions that are similar to what you may face in an upcoming competition. You will experience less nervousness and anxiety if you have already tried out and practiced conditions you will encounter in the actual competition. The simulations will increase your overall confidence and the belief that you can handle anything the competition throws your way. For example, if you are an attacker in volleyball and are getting ready to face a team with outstanding blocking, a worthwhile simulation is to attach a 12- to 18-inch board to the top of the net, then practice spiking over or around that artificial block. As another example, let's say you are a basketball forward preparing to face an opposing team with a very tall center who can block shots extremely well. In this case, you could have a teammate with a tennis racket guard you while you attempt your jump shots in practice. This will help you adjust the arc of your shots to compensate for the tall defender. If you play football and are a quarterback, center, running back, tight end, or wide receiver, it would be a good idea in practice sessions to have the football dunked in water before each snap. This will provide you with confidence when you play in rainy conditions.

Developing useful simulations requires a good deal of shared expertise. Accurate and detailed knowledge of what may actually transpire in competitions can be best developed by working with

By working with your coach, you can likely predict game situations.

your coach, and even other athletes that play the same position as you. Your pooled knowledge can likely predict a large percentage of game situations that may require special attention. By incorporating simulations into your yearly training program, you will feel far more confident that you can handle the difficult situations that invariably arise in competitive sport.

Prepare, prepare, prepare One of the easiest ways to prevent cognitive state anxiety from hurting your performance is to develop a strong sense of self-confidence and self-efficacy. Chapter 2 presents a variety of techniques to do just that. Research indicates that athletes who believe they are completely prepared for competition tend to feel less nervous and anxious. Self-confidence is the perfect anecdote for anxiety. But this self-confidence can be developed and nurtured only if you utilize meticulous preparation in terms of your physical skills, your mental preparation strategies, your cardiovascular endurance, and your game strategy. If you work with the material presented in this chapter, you will be well on your way to taking your game to the next level. But remember, all these interventions must be practiced regularly by incorporating them into your yearly training program.

Prepare!
Prepare!
PREPARE!

Personal Application 4.3 Identifying strategies of personal importance.

Which of the interventions presented in this chapter could benefit your personal sport performance? To answer this question, identify some past competitions when you needed to increase your arousal to be at the top of your game. If you could go back to those moments in time, which strategies would you try first, and why? Then think back to times when you could have really used some help in lowering your arousal and anxiety for maximum performance. Which arousal-reducing strategies do you wish you had tried during those stressful times? Why do you think those particular interventions would work best for you? Finally, outline a specific plan in terms of when and how you are going to experiment with these techniques off-site, in practices, and in preseason games. Be specific, and use the goal-setting guidelines outlined in Chapter 2.

Summary and Conclusions

In this chapter, you learned the importance of the arousal–performance relationship and were given information to help you determine the optimal arousal required for your sport or position. One of the most difficult aspects of competitive sport is handling the stress and anxiety that come with competition. Although every athlete feels "up" or aroused before a contest, cognitive state anxiety will cause your performance to deteriorate drastically if you do not learn how to identify it and handle it properly. The Symptoms of Distress Checklist and the CSAI-2 will give you an idea of your susceptibility to physical and mental stress or anxiety. By being aware of your feelings at an appropriate time, you will be able to implement one or more of the arousal-adjustment strategies presented in this chapter before cognitive anxiety can hurt your performance when it matters most. So take the time to experiment with a variety of these interventions, both off-site and at home, to determine which have the potential to help you perform at the top of your game. Then practice them, practice them, and practice them some more. That way, these strategies will be well established when the competitive season gets under way.

THE ATHLETE'S LIBRARY

Gill, D.L. (1994). A sport and exercise psychology perspective on stress. *Quest, 44,* 20-27.

Krane, V., Joyce, D., & Rafeld, J. (1994). Competitive anxiety, situation criticality, and softball performance. *The Sport Psychologist, 8,* 58-72.

Martens, R., Vealey, R.S., & Burton, D. (1990). *Competitive anxiety in sport.* Champaign, IL: Human Kinetics.

Martin, K.A., Moritz, S.E., & Hall, C.R. (1999). Imagery use in sport: A literature review and applied model. *The Sport Psychologist, 13,* 245-268.

Maynard, I.W., Warwick-Evans, L., & Smith, M.J. (1995). The effects of a cognitive intervention strategy on competitive state anxiety and performance in semiprofessional soccer players. *Journal of Sport and Exercise Psychology, 17,* 428-446.

KEY TERMS

anxiety

arousal

autonomic nervous system

cognitive state anxiety

deep breathing

distress

eustress

5 to 1 count breathing

inverted-U theory

mental rehearsal

optimal arousal

parasympathetic system

positive imagery

somatic state anxiety

state anxiety

stress

sympathetic system

three-part breathing

trait anxiety

CHAPTER CONTENTS

CHAPTER 5

MAINTAINING YOUR ATTENTIONAL FOCUS

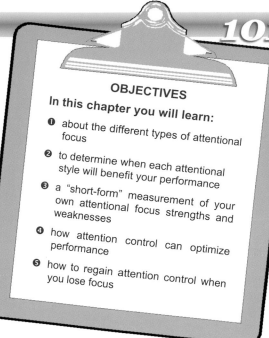

OBJECTIVES

In this chapter you will learn:

❶ about the different types of attentional focus

❷ to determine when each attentional style will benefit your performance

❸ a "short-form" measurement of your own attentional focus strengths and weaknesses

❹ how attention control can optimize performance

❺ how to regain attention control when you lose focus

If you have been playing competitive sports for any length of time, you can almost certainly identify with Steve in the story below. Can you recall a time when you seemed to be coasting toward sure victory, only to have some unforeseen event cause you to come completely "unglued?" If this has ever happened to you, you will recall that all the skills and behaviors that were working perfectly up to that point

Steve is a professional golfer playing in the British Open. This tournament is very special to him because he gets to compete in his native country, with friends and family members in the gallery. With one round to go, he was on top of the leader board and was making some of the best golf shots of his distinguished career. His drives had been long and straight, his long irons were accurate, his approach shots were hugging the pin, and his putts were dropping easily. He felt confident he would soon be sipping champagne from the Claret Jug. On the third tee, Steve unleashed a mammoth drive, about 300 yards straight down the middle of the fairway. It looked as if things were going perfectly as he gave his driver to his personal caddy. At that moment, the caddy informed Steve he had two drivers in his bag, meaning he was carrying one club more than the PGA rules allowed. After some heated discussion, it was established that the second driver had been mistakenly put in the golf bag after some experimentation that morning at the driving range. Neither the caddy nor Steve had checked the number of clubs before the scheduled tee-off time. Normally, this was the duty of the caddy, who admitted his mistake and apologized profusely. Under the rules of golf, this violation meant an automatic two-stroke penalty, dropping Steve from atop the leader board. Although there were still many holes to play in the tournament, Steve seemed to completely unravel at this point. His game fell completely apart, and by the end of the day he was off the first page of the leader board, hopelessly out of contention.

seemed to disappear in a moment's notice. Even worse, you likely started making unforced errors and had no idea how to get your game back on track. The bottom line is that something happened to break your concentration. Sometimes this is caused by design, and other times it is caused by unpredictable events.

For example, in the 1960s, the Japanese revolutionized the game of volleyball by creating the first version of the multiple offense. With this new game plan, spikers attacked from every possible position at the net, rather than just the traditional two sides of the court. These set plays were called, and sets were varied in both height and speed. In addition, spikers would sometimes set, and setters would sometimes spike. In basketball, different zone presses were designed and different offensive and defensive plays implemented. Football introduced the "hurry up" offense, the shotgun quarterback formation, and different zone defenses to confuse the competition. Professional boxers have been known to box "lefty" rather than from their normal stance. Similarly, baseball pitchers will suddenly change their delivery angle, dropping to a sidearm or submarine release. The end result in each of these sports is that the opposing players become overwhelmed with all the new information, change their normal approach, and make unforced errors because their attentional focus has been compromised. This often completely changes the outcome of sporting events.

Your own personal reaction to a sporting event can cause you to lose focus.

Other times, attentional focus can be lost because of isolated events that take place in competitive sports—or your reaction to those events. For example, a tennis player who is called for a foot fault on a critical point or who receives a bad call from a line judge, can lose concentration in a matter of seconds. A talented hockey player can be thrown off his usual game plan by being goaded into a fight by a less-skilled competitor. An untimely comment by a teammate can cause you to obsessively focus on the remark rather than on your normal task-relevant factors. Finally, you can become distracted by a family member or friend in the audience.

Because of these and other noteworthy examples, few topics in sport psychology have received as much attention as concentration, or attentional control. Most top-level and elite athletes would agree that focus is often the deciding factor in competitive sport. This chapter gives you a thorough understanding of attentional control and provides you with the necessary tools to avoid performance drop-off caused by the loss of focus. You will also be given a psychometric measure to identify your particular attentional strengths and weaknesses. But before we do this, let's look at the four different types of attention.

Types of Attentional Focus

Regardless of whether you are an athlete or not, every person uses four different types of attention, or concentration, over the course of a day. Each of these is valuable under certain circumstances. So if your coach tells you to concentrate, you need to be keenly aware of the type of concentration that is best suited for that situation. To help you do this, you must realize that attention can be broken down into two distinct categories of focus.

The first category involves the concept of width. Sometimes it is important to maintain a relatively broad focus of attention because you need to evaluate a large number of environmental

ATTENTIONAL FOCUS VARIES BY WIDTH AND DIRECTION.

stimuli. At other times, you need to narrow your attention, focusing your concentration on only a few environmental cues. The second category refers to the concept of direction. Certain situations require you to focus your attention internally, where you concentrate on your personal thoughts and feelings. Other times, your attention must be directed externally to cues in your sporting environment. When these two categories are combined, they produce four different attentional styles. You will use each in your sporting efforts, but they will be used at different times. Before you learn more about these attentional styles, take a few moments to examine Figure 5.1. This will help you visualize the relationship between the four attentional styles.

Broad Internal Focus

A broad internal focus helps you organize and comprehend large amounts of information, recall past situations, or plan for future events. As an athlete, you do this when you honestly assess your strengths and weaknesses to determine your future goals. For example, you rely on a broad internal focus when you prepare your yearly training plan. In doing this, you need to consider your overall fitness and skill levels, your basic understanding of game strategy, your day-to-day motivation concerns, and your ability to employ the mental training principles outlined in this book.

Broad internal focus helps you make sense of large amounts of information.

If you are a football quarterback who calls his or her own plays, you need to rely heavily on broad internal focus to select a play option in the huddle. Your correct choice will be determined by your knowledge of play options, player matchups, and past successes and failures with the different options, and even by an educated feel for what the opposing team may be expecting under the current circumstances. If you are the captain of a team sport, it is necessary to consider each and every athlete's strengths and weaknesses, as well as their personality makeups, to determine the best

Figure 5.1 Attentional focus varies as a function of direction and width.

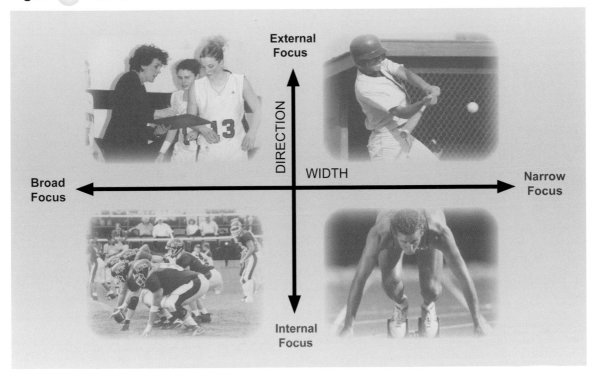

leadership strategy for upcoming competitions. In both these examples, you will notice that a large amount of information is required to help the athlete make the right decision.

Broad External Focus

Broad external focus allows you to "read" a complex environment.

A broad external focus is required to assess, and react to, a complex environmental situation relatively quickly. If you have ever had a summer job as a camp director, or were the coach of a youth sports team, you likely relied heavily on this focus. Hockey legend Wayne Gretzky was known for his amazing ability to assess the development of a play, read the positioning of all players, and then avoid defenders by finding the open man with a perfect pass. Similarly, if you are a point guard in basketball, you need to make a rapid assessment of both teammates and opposing players before executing a set play. Finally, your coach uses this attentional style often as he or she monitors the competition and makes the necessary adjustments over the course of the contest. The common denominator in each of these examples is that a relatively large amount of information needs to be processed quickly to come up with the best possible strategy and response.

Narrow Internal Focus

A **narrow internal focus** is used in situations where you are required to direct your attention inward, such as assessing possible symptoms of distress or using imagery or mental rehearsal. This is an excellent strategy to employ if you need to relax. The breathing and relaxation strategies you learned in the last chapter require narrow internal focus. For example, if you are completing the Symptoms of Distress Checklist, you need to attend to your bodily sensations, such as sweaty palms, increased heart rate, or faster breathing. Similarly, when you use positive imagery or mental rehearsal, you need to focus your attention on a series of mental cues ("moving pictures"). Finally, taking a deep breath before reacting to a less than positive comment from your coach is an example of using narrow internal focus.

Narrow internal focus is perfect for imagery and mental rehearsal.

Narrow External Focus

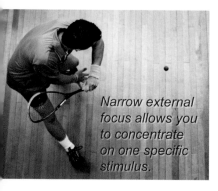

Narrow external focus allows you to concentrate on one specific stimulus.

A **narrow external focus** is used in situations where you are required to react (especially physically) to a particular situation in your sporting environment. When this happens, it is necessary for you to focus your attention toward one or a very small number of external cues. For example, if you are batting in baseball, you need to focus your attention strictly on the baseball throughout the pitcher's delivery. If squash is your game, you need to concentrate specifically on the ball and the opponent's positioning. When playing hockey, if you are lucky enough to be awarded a penalty shot, your concentration will be focused predominantly on the puck, the goalie, and the goal dimensions. As a last example, when your coach or assistant coach is demonstrating a new play or game strategy, you need to direct all your attention to the instructions being given. In each of these cases, it is absolutely imperative that you tune out all other events that are going on around you. You also need to tune out all internal thoughts so you can give the task (or the coach) your complete attention.

Personal Application 5.1 Self-assessment of when each attentional style is required in your sport.

Take a few moments to identify several examples of when each of the four attentional styles is required in your sport of choice. Be as specific as possible in your analysis.

Broad internal focus is required when I:

➢ _____

➢ _____

➢ _____

Broad external focus is required when I:

➢ _____

➢ _____

➢ _____

Narrow internal focus is required when I:

➢ _____

➢ _____

➢ _____

Narrow external focus is required when I:

➢ _____

➢ _____

➢ _____

The Measurement of Attentional Style

Fortunately, a good deal of research has led to the development of a psychometric instrument for measuring attentional style. This tool is called the Attentional Style Inventory. A mini version of the instrument that can be completed in a relatively short period of time is provided here. The mini version measures six scales that have particular relevance for any athlete. The major reason to consider taking this test is that it allows you to identify your "relative" strengths and weaknesses in terms of attentional focus. The word *relative* is used because the test only allows you to establish a rank ordering of the different dimensions.

Your test scores are a valuable tool that can be used in developing a personal performance improvement plan. The Attentional Style Inventory is provided for your use in Table 5.1. Remember that there are no right or wrong answers to the questions. By understanding your predominant strengths and weaknesses, you will be better able to predict the types of mistakes you are likely to commit under pressure. This advanced warning can give you an important "heads up" on preventing or minimizing the effects of your attentional weaknesses.

This inventory was revised specifically for this book, with the sole intention of providing a quick and easy tool for assessing your relative strengths and weaknesses in attentional style. This means that no psychometric properties are available for the test. The questions were adapted and modified from the conceptual framework described earlier in this chapter and referenced in The Athlete's Library.

IT'S TIME TO IDENTIFY YOUR PREDOMINANT ATTENTIONAL STYLE.

Scoring the Attentional Style Inventory

When scoring your inventory, please note that two questions are included in each subscale. Add your scores from the combined total of the following pairs of questions to get the overall subscale totals:

BET total = questions 1 + 2   **OET total** = questions 3 + 4

BIT total = questions 5 + 6   OIT total = questions 7 + 8
NAR total = questions 9 + 10   RED total = questions 11 + 12

Table 5.1 Attentional Style Inventory.

Attentional Style Inventory

<u>Directions</u>: A number of statements are provided below. Read each one carefully, then circle the number that most clearly describes how much it applies to you. Don't spend too much time on each question, because your first response is likely correct. There are no right or wrong answers, so be honest.

		Never	Rarely	Sometimes	Frequently	Always
1.	In my sport, I have the ability to quickly "read" a play that is developing.	0	1	2	3	4
2.	At the gymnasium, arena, or playing field, I know what each of my teammates is doing at any point in time.	0	1	2	3	4
3.	When listening to my coach or a teammate talk, I tend to get distracted by other sights or sounds.	0	1	2	3	4
4.	I tend to feel overwhelmed when I watch sports where several things are happening at once.	0	1	2	3	4
5.	I can come up with a large number or ideas from a relatively small amount of information.	0	1	2	3	4
6.	I am good at "tying together" information from a variety of sources, such as feedback from coaches or assistant coaches.	0	1	2	3	4
7.	When listening to others talk, I tend to become distracted by my own thoughts and ideas.	0	1	2	3	4
8.	I become forgetful because I have so many things on my mind.	0	1	2	3	4
9.	It is easy for me to "tune out" my thoughts while focusing on a particular play, event, or discussion.	0	1	2	3	4
10.	It is easy for me to "tune out" other sights and sounds while focusing on a particular thought or idea.	0	1	2	3	4
11.	It is hard to get a single thought or idea out of my head.	0	1	2	3	4
12.	I make mistakes because I focus too much on one thing.	0	1	2	3	4

Each subscale can have a score ranging from 0 to 8. To visualize the representation of your profile, plot your scores in Table 5.2.

To plot the scores, place an X over the number on the broad external line that is the same as your BET score. Then place an X over the number on the broad internal line that is the same as your BIT score. Next, place an X over the number that represents your NAR score on both the narrow external and narrow internal lines. These X scores represent your attentional strengths. The higher your number, the greater the attentional strength. Look to see if one of the lines has a much larger X number than the others. If so, this category represents your most predominant attentional style.

The scores for the scales that represent **attentional errors** can be plotted in a similar fashion. Place an O over the number on the broad external line that is the same as your score for OET. Then place an O over the number on the broad internal line that is the same as your OIT score. Next, place an O over the number that represents your RED score on both the narrow external and narrow internal lines. Once again, look to see if one of the lines has a much larger O score than the others. If so, this represents your attentional style that is most susceptible to attentional errors.

The inventory will help you identify likely attentional errors that may hinder your performance.

Table 5.2 Schematic profile of your Attentional Style Inventory.

Broad External	1	2	3	4	5	6	7	8
Broad Internal	1	2	3	4	5	6	7	8
Narrow External	1	2	3	4	5	6	7	8
Narrow Internal	1	2	3	4	5	6	7	8

As previously mentioned, the line with the highest X number represents your predominant attentional style. Of special importance to you as a competitive athlete, however, is the fact that the line (subscale) with the highest total of both the X and O numbers represents your attentional style that can, under pressure, become the most serious problem. For example, if your total combined score for X and O numbers is highest in the broad internal dimension, then you may be prone to making mistakes because you become distracted (lose focus) by too much unnecessary information in the sporting environment.

Subscale Definitions and Scoring Interpretation

BET total This refers to your broad external focus of attention. If you received a high X score on this subscale, you have the ability to process and deal with a large amount of information at one time.

OET total This represents an overload due to external information. If you scored a high O on this dimension, it indicates that you are prone to making mistakes because you become distracted by too much irrelevant information going on around you.

BIT total This indicates a broad internal focus of attention. If this is your highest X score, it suggests you have an excellent ability to analyze and make long-term plans. People scoring high on this dimension usually have excellent intellectual and organizational skills.

OIT total This reveals an overload caused by internal information. A high O score in this category indicates you are prone to making mistakes because you tend to become distracted by your own thoughts or ideas.

NAR total This category represents a narrow focus of attention. If you scored a high X on the narrow external subscale, you likely have an excellent ability to concentrate or focus on one specific thing. You also tend to be a very well-disciplined and dedicated athlete.

RED total This reveals an over-reduced focus of attention. If you have a high O score on this subscale, you probably have the tendency to narrow your attention too much. This will cause you to perform at a lower level in highly charged or important competitive situations.

Personal Application 5.2 Self-awareness of your own particular attentional strengths and weaknesses.

As a self-awareness exercise, take a few minutes to complete the Attentional Style Inventory outlined in Table 5.1. Then, score the test as indicated in the text. Remember to be completely honest in your responses so that this exercise can help you become a better athlete.

What is your major attentional strength, as indicated by the inventory? Provide some examples of when this strength is most evident in your sport performance.

_____

_____

_____

_____

What was your lowest attentional score, as indicated by the inventory? When could this particular attentional style help you in your athletic pursuits?

_____

_____

_____

_____

When you come under pressure, what particular attentional style is most likely to cause you problems (the highest X and O total)? Can you think of times when this has happened in your competitions?

_____

_____

_____

_____

_____

_____

_____

To reiterate, it is very important for you to realize that the Attentional Style Inventory is only a mini inventory, meaning it is a short form of a longer version. It will, however, provide you with an excellent starting point for identifying your predominant attentional style, as well as the attentional style that may cause you the most problems in competition.

Principles of Attention–Control Training for Optimal Performance

You can use attention-control training to be your absolute best.

At this point in the chapter, you are most likely wondering what major implications can be drawn from completed research in the field of sport psychology. Several consistent trends seem to have particular relevance for any athlete wanting to elevate his or her performance to the next level of excellence. We now take a few moments to examine some of these principles. Each one demonstrates the value of attention-control training.

You must be able to engage in all four types of attentional focus

Participation in competitive sports presents you with several unique and difficult challenges. Athletic contests are complex, fast moving, constantly changing, tiring, and very stressful. In addition, your skills in most sports, but particularly in team sports, must be performed in conjunction with team members, competitors, coaches, referees, and even spectators. All these factors require you to be able to instantly shift your focus (concentration) to the most appropriate attentional style for any particular situation. Learning to do this requires knowledge and practice with attention-control training.

Different competitive situations present you with different attentional demands

There will be times in your sport when you need to attend to a large number of external and internal cues. For example, if you are a soccer goalie, you need to "read" the development

Learn to adjust your attentional style.

of an offensive play by the opposing team. Then you must mentally review the offensive options, your team's defensive strategy, the relative strengths and weaknesses of the opponents, and any past tendencies from previous encounters. At this point in time, to perform at your best, you cannot allow yourself to be distracted by your opponents, your teammates, or even the spectators. This requires you to make an immediate shift from broad external to broad internal focus. Once you have reviewed your options, you need to once again shift your attentional focus—this time from broad internal to narrow external concentration. At this point, you will focus exclusively on the soccer ball, and you should never take your eyes off it. Although this shift from broad external to broad internal to narrow external represents a relatively extreme example, all athletes need to develop this capacity to shift attentional focus as the situation demands.

Under optimal conditions, most athletes find it quite easy to meet different attentional demands

When you are participating in relaxed practice sessions or exhibition contests, you probably don't find it difficult to shift your attentional focus back and forth between the four different attentional styles. Listening to your coach, relating with your teammates, focusing on a new skill or play demonstration, and even using imagery to imagine yourself performing that new skill or play flawlessly all require different attentional styles. The point is that under relaxed conditions, these shifts are easy, but as you well know, competitive sport does not usually offer these optimal circumstances.

Important competitions result in increased pressure that will interfere with your ability to maintain the mental flexibility to shift attentional styles

In the previous chapter, you learned that too much arousal can cause your performance to deteriorate tremendously. A growing body of research in sport psychology now indicates that excessive arousal has the same negative effect on your ability to make quick shifts in attentional style. This means that in the heat of competition, you are likely to experience difficulties in making the necessary shifts in focus. This, in turn, will hinder your overall performance. Something seems to happen in competition that doesn't happen in practice sessions or low-key contests.

Even before you become aware that you are feeling pressure, you will begin to rely more exclusively on your own particular attentional strength

As your arousal continues to build and move out of the moderate range, your own personal attentional strength will kick in and take over. For example, if you identified narrow internal as your major attentional strength in Personal Application 5.2, this attentional style will become more dominant as pressure mounts—and more predictive of how you will perform in that situation. The fact that it has become more dominant means you will find it much more difficult to shift your attentional styles as dictated by the athletic event. In this particular case, your heavy reliance on narrow internal focus will likely prevent you from recognizing important cues in the athletic contest. In other words, you may continue to mentally rehearse a particular move when that move is no longer working. This will have the negative effect of causing you to repeat the same mistake over and over again.

PRESSURE HINDERS YOUR ABILITY TO SHIFT ATTENTIONAL FOCUS.

An athlete's "default position" is his or her attentional strength.

With increasing pressure, your attentional focus will start to narrow

In any competition, many cues will be available for processing. Under conditions of low arousal, you will probably be able to identify both relevant and irrelevant cues. When your arousal level is low, irrelevant cues will almost certainly hinder your performance. For example, if you see a boyfriend, girlfriend, or parent in the audience, you will tend to be distracted from the task-relevant factors that are crucial to your success. Then, as your arousal level increases to an optimal level, you will begin to experience attentional narrowing. This causes you to "gate out," or ignore, all the irrelevant cues while focusing completely on the relevant ones. This is a good thing. It results in a great performance because you eliminate all environmental cues that are irrelevant to the proper execution of your skill. But if your arousal continues to increase past your optimal level, your attention will continue to narrow even more, resulting in your gating out even the relevant cues in the athletic contest. If this happens, your performance will deteriorate almost immediately.

When arousal is low, it is easier to become distracted by irrelevent cues.

Under competitive pressure, if you notice physical symptoms, such as faster heart rate, a nervous stomach, or sweaty palms, your attention will become more internally focused

When you start to notice these and other physical symptoms, you will almost invariably become less attentive to important changes in the competition and the all-important task-relevant factors. At this point in time, you will be far more likely to make a mistake. But to make matters even worse, this increasing narrow internal focusing will cause you to experience competitive state anxiety. Most researchers believe this occurs because you are becoming increasingly aware that you are feeling nervous. When this happens, you start to feel that something is definitely wrong and that you may not be up for the challenge. This increase in competitive anxiety is very problematic, as you learned in the last chapter, and it will cause your performance to drop off drastically if you don't have a strategy for reversing the process.

Attention-Control Training Strategies for Regaining Focus

If you want to continue your quest to take your performance to the next level, then it is absolutely essential that you learn how to focus your attention in the most appropriate manner. Earlier in this chapter, you learned about the relative advantages and disadvantages of each attentional style. In Personal Application 5.2, you performed an assessment to determine your own particular attentional strengths and weaknesses. Now that you are armed with that information, it is time to look at how you can move back and forth between the attentional styles that are most appropriate for different sporting circumstances.

One of the most difficult problems you will face is eliminating those nagging negative thoughts that invariably crop up during an athletic competition and replacing them with positive thoughts and self-statements. It is completely natural to experience feelings of worry and self-doubt at critical times in the contest. But the fact remains that you will either regain attentional focus and perform successfully or those self-defeating thoughts will cause your performance to deteriorate significantly. This fact highlights the importance of learning how to use selective attention to regain attentional control at critical times. This section offers an excellent strategy that has helped many elite athletes eliminate negative thoughts and ultimately regain attentional focus. The intervention is composed of two distinct elements: thought stopping and centering. Both techniques prove to be reliable mental tools.

You need to match your attentional focus with what the situation requires.

Thought Stopping

It is critical that you approach every contest with the belief that you will succeed in your efforts. In those times when you need to regain your attentional focus, you must learn how to stop negative thoughts and replace them with positive thoughts. You were exposed to this concept in Chapter 2, where you learned how to recognize cognitive distortions and turn them into internal dialogue that could improve your performance. All this information still applies, but there is one special attention-control strategy that has great potential when you think you are losing focus. Psychologists call this process **thought stopping**.

Thought stopping is a great technique for regaining focus.

Psychological theory tells us that you will not be able to give your complete attention to any more than one attention-demanding task at a time. This means it is impossible to attend to a negative thought or self-statement and still perform at your optimal level. In other words, any negative thought needs to be immediately stopped and replaced. Interviews with a large number of elite athletes have led to many valuable techniques for doing just that. For example, visualizing a stop sign and repeating self-statements such as "Stop this kind of thinking—you know you can execute this skill perfectly" or "Danger, danger—don't go there" have proven highly effective.

Centering

Once you have successfully stopped the negative thought, it will be possible for you to center your attention internally. For obvious reasons, this stage is referred to as **centering**. Centering has a way of directly countering many of the changes that accompany a loss of your attentional control. Within the space of a few seconds, you will be able to calm down and accurately assess the current situation,

LOSING IT!

Jeremy Wotherspoon, the most dominant male long-track speedskater of the past decade, winner of more World Cup medals than any other man in history, and a four-time world sprint champion allowed anger to cheat him out of a medal in the 2006 Winter Olympics in Turin, Italy. In the 500-meter event, Wotherspoon performed far below his capabilities in the first heat. In this event, the times from two races are combined to determine the winner. After the first race, Wotherspoon was within three-hundredths of a second of a bronze medal, but instead of focusing on the podium, he allowed his anger about the previous race to defeat him. In the second race, he finished a dismal 17th, giving him a 9th-place finish overall. After the race, he was quoted as saying, "In every part of the race, there are specific things that you focus on. . . . I've been having problems with the turns. Especially the turn in the 500. It's mostly a mental thing where, as soon as I get close to the first turn, I start to think 'I don't know what this is going to feel like.' Because of that, I subconsciously back off." This was clearly a case of an athlete, under pressure, "thinking himself stupid." In this situation, Wotherspoon should have maintained his attentional focus and concentrated on the mechanics of his race. As an elite athlete, his muscle memory and instincts should have been allowed to take the lead. There will be plenty of time to think about it now!

then redirect your focus in an appropriate way. This strategy is highly effective, but it will work only if you follow two very important guidelines. First and foremost, remember to take the time needed to center. Second, it is imperative that you know where to redirect your focus once you have regained attentional control. To take full advantage of this procedure, you need to become completely conscious of your center of gravity. The following guidelines will help you accomplish the centering procedure:

▶ Start with your feet slightly apart and your knees partially bent. Your weight should be equally balanced between both feet. You can test this by first leaning forward, then backward, then side to side. Focus on your weight, shifting with each move but coming back to a central, balanced position.

▶ At this point, consciously relax your neck and shoulder muscles. You can check this relaxation by moving your head slightly forward, backward, and side to side. Very gently, shake your hands and arms to make sure they feel loose and relaxed.

▶ Keep your mouth open slightly to reduce tension in your jaw muscles.

▶ Concentrate on breathing in from the diaphragm, then out with the abdomen. As you inhale slowly, focus on two sets of cues. First, notice that your abdomen is extending with your inhalation. Second, consciously maintain the feeling of relaxation in your neck and shoulder muscles. This deep breathing, as you have already learned in Chapter 4, will counter the tendency for you to tense your neck and shoulder muscles.

Centering will help you calm down and regain focus.

▶ Focus on exhaling slowly. As you do so, pay special attention to the increased feeling of relaxation as your abdominal muscles contract. Then allow your knees to bend a bit more as you experience an increased feeling of heaviness as your weight presses down toward the ground. At this point, pay attention to the fact that your entire body feels more steady and "planted." The bottom line is that as you consciously focus on each of these relaxing physical cues, you

Personal Application 5.3   Your first practice with the thought-stopping and centering intervention.

The next time you experience a loss of attentional focus, take a few seconds to experiment with this technique. It is best to perform this initial practice off-site, not during an actual competition. You need to work out the bugs before you try implementing this strategy in an important contest. Try this at home, at school, or at work when you feel your attention has been broken.

will automatically stop thinking about all those things that initially caused you to lose attentional control in the first place.

The centering procedure needs to be practiced on a regular basis, so remember to include it in your yearly training program. Over time, within the space of a single breath, you will learn how to lower your level of arousal and redirect your attentional focus to the most relevant cues in your sporting environment.

Summary and Conclusions

Attention control is one of the most important psychological skills in competitive athletics. Sports take place in an ever-changing, complex, dynamic, and highly stressful environment. This means your attentional focus will need to change many times during any competition or even practice. So although there will be many opportunities for the taking, there will also be many potential pitfalls that can hinder your performance. To help you take advantage of those opportunities—and avoid the pitfalls—this chapter provides the most recent research in the area of attention-control training.

To begin this process, you learned about several different types of attentional focus and how each attentional style is appropriate at different times in competitive sport. Each of these attentional strengths can create attentional errors that will invariably hurt your performance. To identify your own particular strengths and weaknesses, fill out the Attentional Style Inventory, score it as directed, and then complete a self-assessment exercise regarding your predominant attentional style, as well as your attentional style that can, under pressure, become a serious weakness. The chapter offers seven specific principles of attention-control training and concludes by describing a highly effective intervention for regaining your attentional focus at critical times. The thought-stopping and centering strategy has been used successfully by many elite and professional athletes around the world. So take the time to learn this technique, then watch your overall performance continue to soar.

THE ATHLETE'S LIBRARY

Cox, R.H. (2002). *Sport psychology: Concepts and applications*. New York: McGraw-Hill.

Nideffer, R.M. (1995). *Focus for success*. San Diego: Enhanced Performance Services.

Nideffer, R.M., Sagal, M.S., Lowry, M., & Bond, J. (2000). Identifying and developing world class performers. In *The practice of sport and exercise psychology: International perspectives* (pp. 129-144). Morgantown, WV: Fitness Information Technology.

Ziegler, S.G. (1994). The effects of attentional shift training on the execution of soccer skills: A preliminary investigation. *Journal of Applied Behavioral Analysis, 27,* 545-552.

KEY TERMS

attentional errors

attentional focus

Attentional Style Inventory

broad external focus

broad internal focus

centering

focus direction

focus width

narrow external focus

narrow internal focus

thought stopping

CHAPTER CONTENTS

CHAPTER 6

INTERPRETING YOUR SUCCESSES AND FAILURES

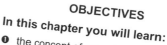

OBJECTIVES

In this chapter you will learn:

❶ the concept of causal attribution

❷ a self-assessment tool to identify your own typical attributions

❸ how locus of control attributions and stability attributions affect you

❹ the value of attributional training for you personally

❺ guidelines that will help make causal attributions work for you in your sport

In the following scenario, it is interesting how the same hockey game could result in such different interpretations of the unexpected loss. These completely different explanations likely leave you with some very important questions. For example, why do athletes feel the need to analyze their competitive efforts? How is it possible that the same

A high school hockey team that was currently undefeated in league play was facing an opponent with a very poor win–loss record. Right from the first face-off, it was apparent that the league leaders were not performing up to their usual level of excellence. Not one of the shifts was finishing plays, skating hard, or playing two-way hockey. It looked as if they were just waiting for the other team to hand them their expected victory. At the end of a scoreless first period, the coach had some choice comments for his athletes. He told them he was ashamed of their effort and pointed out that they were playing with "absolutely no heart." He further warned that if they didn't elevate their level of play immediately, a serious upset could be in the making. In spite of the coach's warning, the team continued to play as if just going through the motions. This trend continued late into the third period, and the game remained scoreless. With just under five minutes to play, the referee awarded a penalty shot to a member of the opposing team. The shot was successful, and the undefeated team was in serious danger of recording its first loss. At this point, their overall level of play picked up noticeably, but they were unable to make a comeback, losing their first game of the season. After the contest, the team members offered a variety of opinions to explain the loss. About half the team blamed the loss on a "stupid call" by the referee. Several other players had praise for the opposing team, suggesting they were better than their record indicated. One player secretly blamed the coach, and a handful of athletes blamed the loss on a lack of effort.

EVERY ATHLETE FEELS THE NEED TO ANALYZE PAST PERFORMANCES.

sporting experience could be viewed in such different ways? What effect do these different explanations have on a competitor's mood or emotions? Does the nature of interpretation regarding the outcome have an effect on future motivation to improve performance? And finally, what effect does the athlete's perception have on expectancies for future successes or failures?

In this chapter, we draw exclusively from the sport psychology literature on causal attribution to provide some answers to these important questions. Even more important, we offer a variety of recommendations that will help you develop honest interpretations for your successes and failures. The net result is that you will feel better about your competitive efforts and your desire to elevate your game, leaving you feeling much better about your chances for future success. In the final analysis, you will have all the attributional tools to take your performance to the next level.

Understanding Causal Attribution

Causal attributions are strong motivators.

The notion of causal attribution theory can be best described as a cognitive approach to motivation. This means that how you view different situations can seriously affect the intensity of your quest to get better. The underlying principle of this theory is that all individuals have the need to explain, understand, and predict events based on their own personal perceptions. When applied to the world of competitive sport, this means you will experience a strong need to make sense of your sporting experiences. To better understand this phenomenon, you will find it helpful to complete the self-assessment exercise in Personal Application 6.1.

The key element of attribution theory is perception. This means that your explanations for past successes and failures may be entirely incorrect, but that is not the main point. What really matters is what you believe to be true. There is an old saying that "no one really perceives reality—we interpret what we see and call it reality." For this reason, it is important that you have a thorough

Personal Application 6.1 Self-analysis of causal attributions you have used.

Think back over the past competitive season. What are some of the common explanations you have used to explain successful and unsuccessful experiences? Once again, be completely honest in your analysis.

Explanations I have given for successful performances:

➢ _____

➢ _____

➢ _____

➢ _____

➢ _____

➢ _____

Explanations I have given for unsuccessful performances:

➢ _____

➢ _____

➢ _____

➢ _____

➢ _____

➢ _____

understanding of the nature of causal attributions and how those attributions can affect your future motivation, your expectancy, and ultimately your performance.

Regardless of the explanations you have endorsed in the past, research suggests there is a specific pattern to how you formulate these attributions. In the next section, you will learn about the most frequent categories of causal attribution.

The Basic Causal Attribution Scheme

Carl Lewis was an exceptional sprinter. Was it ability, effort, task difficulty, or luck? How would he answer?

The earliest research on the basic causal attribution scheme demonstrates that when individuals are in achievement situations, they invariably attempt to explain why the particular outcome occurred. In other words, why were they successful or unsuccessful, or why did they win or lose? You do the same thing in your competitive sport—you strive to make sense of the outcome. This same body of research concludes that people generally draw on four categories of explanation: their own *ability*, their own *effort*, the *difficulty of the task*, and the degree of good or bad *luck* experienced.

Later stages of research take these four categories and organize them into two major dimensions. First, the locus of control dimension distinguishes between the combined *internal* factors of ability and effort and the combined *external* factors of task difficulty and luck. Second, the stability dimension distinguishes between the combined *stable* factors of ability and task difficulty and the combined *unstable* factors of effort and luck. Although this probably sounds confusing to you at the moment, you will easily understand the relationships once you have examined the classification scheme in Table 6.1.

YOU ARE IN CONTROL OF YOUR EFFORT ON A DAY-TO-DAY BASIS.

From Table 6.1, you can see that ability is classified as a stable internal factor, while effort is classified as an unstable internal factor. Both your ability and effort are completely personal, or internal in nature. However, effort is constantly changing (i.e., unstable), while your ability is relatively unchanging (i.e., stable). For example, if you are a squash player, your overall level of ability does not change much from one match to the next, but the effort you put out on any given day can vary dramatically.

Conversely, task difficulty and luck are totally external in terms of your locus of control (i.e., they are both completely beyond your control). However, the ability of your opponent (task difficulty) is

Table 6.1 The classification scheme for causal attributions.

| | | LOCUS OF CONTROL | |
		Internal	External
STABILITY	**Stable**	Ability	Task Difficulty
	Unstable	Effort	Luck

relatively stable and unchanging, while your luck is unstable and ever changing. For example, an opposing hockey team's level of ability is going to be relatively consistent from one game to the next, since it involves a sum total of all the players' skills. But in one game, your team may get a bad call from the referee and a shot may hit the crossbar, while on another day, the calls and bounces can go completely your way.

Within this four-choice framework, the bottom line is that you will usually attribute your successful or unsuccessful performances to one of the four factors of ability, effort, task difficulty, or luck. Take a few moments now to review Table 6.2, and see if you have ever used these or similar explanations after a competitive event.

Feel free to insert some of the most common attributions you have endorsed under each category. This will make the table even more meaningful to you.

Although you can get a pretty good idea about the type of attributions you normally endorse, it is a good idea to take a more direct measure to be sure of your natural attribution tendencies. The next section gives you a personalized test to do just that.

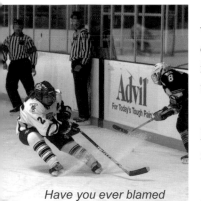

Have you ever blamed external factors such as officiating for an unsuccessful outcome?

Table 6.2 Common causal attributions used by athletes.

Ability Attributes

"I played terribly today, and I deserved to lose."
"I was at the absolute top of my game the whole contest."
"My defensive skills are really starting to pay big dividends."
"I wasn't mentally prepared for this match, and it showed."

➢ _____

➢ _____

Effort Attributes

"This competition went great because I have been putting out in practice."
"I didn't leave anything in the locker room today. I played with heart."
"I didn't play with enough intensity today."
"My whole performance was completely flat."

➢ _____

➢ _____

Task Difficulty/Opponent's Ability Attributes

"I lost to a better competitor today."
"I won my race today, but it was a weak field and my time was too slow."
"No one could put a shot past that goalie today the way he/she was playing."
"Nobody thought I could win today, but I proved them wrong."

➢ _____

➢ _____

Luck Attributes

"I only won because my opponent false-started."
"I never play well in the wind and rain."
"If the puck hadn't bounced over my stick on that breakaway, we would have won."
"Why did we have to meet that team in the first round? They always beat us."

➢ _____

➢ _____

Measuring Your Own Causal Attribution Tendencies

There will be times when you play your best but lose to someone better.

Ongoing research has provided us with a variety of psychometric instruments to measure causal attribution directly. Generally speaking, the large number of tests can be broken down into two categories. The first category is the structural rating scale. With this type of measurement, you are asked to rate several attributions in terms of their impact on an event. Traditionally, winning or losing was the event measured, but lately this has changed to successful or unsuccessful outcomes. This distinction is important because there will be times when you play your very best but still lose to a superior opponent.

As an experienced athlete, you will undoubtedly agree that playing your best always represents a successful outcome. On the other side of the coin, there will be times when you play beneath your usual standards of performance but win anyway because of an inferior or poorly prepared opponent. Most athletes will agree that this scenario represents an unsuccessful outcome. This distinction not only provides a more realistic picture but also serves to better maintain your motivation over the course of the season. This is why you learned about the advantages of performance and process goals over outcome goals in Chapter 3.

The list of attributions used in the structural rating scale usually includes the four categories of ability, effort, task difficulty, and luck. Each attribute is then rated along a numerical scale in terms of how much each category contributed to your successful or unsuccessful outcome. Table 6.3 provides a sample measurement instrument to determine the nature of your attributions.

This causal attribution survey will give you a good idea of what you believe is responsible for your successful and unsuccessful performances in competitive sport. With the information provided in the remainder of this section, you will be able to use your answers as a springboard for discussion with your coach or as a focus on attributional training that may benefit your future efforts.

Table 6.3 A sample test to measure your causal attributions.

Causal Attribution Survey

Two situations are presented below: a successful sport performance (situation A) and an unsuccessful sport performance (situation B). To complete this survey, it is necessary for you to recall two such sporting experiences. Record each situation, then indicate the degree to which each of the attributes of ability, effort, task (opponent) difficulty, and luck was a factor in those outcomes.

Situation A: Successful Outcome

Describe the successful outcome: _____

	Not at All		Somewhat			Very Much So	
1. To what extent do you feel your personal skill or ability was a factor in the successful outcome?	1	2	3	4	5	6	7
2. To what extent do you feel your tremendous effort was a factor in the successful outcome?	1	2	3	4	5	6	7
3. To what extent do you feel your opponent's lack of ability was a factor in the successful outcome?	1	2	3	4	5	6	7
4. To what extent do you feel your good luck was a factor in the successful outcome?	1	2	3	4	5	6	7

Situation B: Unsuccessful Outcome

Describe the unsuccessful outcome: _____

	Not at All		Somewhat			Very Much So	
5. To what extent do you feel your personal skill or ability was a factor in the unsuccessful outcome?	1	2	3	4	5	6	7
6. To what extent do you feel your lack of effort was a factor in the unsuccessful outcome?	1	2	3	4	5	6	7
7. To what extent do you feel your opponent's high ability was a factor in the unsuccessful outcome?	1	2	3	4	5	6	7
8. To what extent do you feel your bad luck was a factor in the unsuccessful outcome?	1	2	3	4	5	6	7

A second technique for measuring causal attribution is the **open-ended measurement** system. This technique can be highly effective because it does not put words in your mouth, as is the case with the causal attribution survey. With this measurement strategy, you are asked to formulate your own attributions and then rate them on a numerical scale, indicating their relative importance in determining your competitive outcome. The main advantage is that you may list factors other than ability, effort, task difficulty, and luck. This open-ended technique allows you to express your perceptions in your own words. When you have time, complete Personal Application 6.2, and determine your own explanations for different outcomes.

Now that you have the tools for determining your most frequent causal attributions, it is important to turn your focus to the major implications and relevance of these important perceptions. We do this by analyzing the locus of control and stability dimensions separately.

How Locus of Control Attributions Affect You

Sport psychology research provides us with an excellent understanding of the relative importance of internal versus external attributions in athletics. Here you will learn the relevance and importance of these attributions in your competitive efforts.

Most athletes tend to be egocentric when making their attributions

One of the most important things for you to know is that you will not always be logical in interpreting your sport performances. This is because almost everyone uses self-serving explanations to interpret outcomes. For example, research repeatedly demonstrates that individuals will invariably attribute successful outcomes to internal causes, while unsuccessful outcomes are seen as the result of external factors. This tendency to attribute successful outcomes to internal factors is called an **ego-enhancing strategy**,

Personal Application 6.2 An open-ended measurement of causal attributions.

Causal Attribution Survey

To use this open-ended measurement technique, you are once again asked to consider a recent successful outcome (situation A) and an unsuccessful outcome (situation B). Try to recall these events in as much detail as possible, then list any factors that you think caused the successful and unsuccessful outcomes. Circle the number that indicates how important you believe each factor was in determining the overall outcome of the contest.

Situation A: Successful Outcome

Describe the successful outcome: _____

	Not at All		Somewhat			Very Much So	
Factor #1 _____	1	2	3	4	5	6	7
Factor #2 _____	1	2	3	4	5	6	7
Factor #3 _____	1	2	3	4	5	6	7

Situation B: Unsuccessful Outcome

Describe the unsuccessful outcome: _____

	Not at All		Somewhat			Very Much So	
Factor #1 _____	1	2	3	4	5	6	7
Factor #2 _____	1	2	3	4	5	6	7
Factor #3 _____	1	2	3	4	5	6	7

Self-serving attributions can hinder your performance if used repeatedly.

while explaining away your unsuccessful performances to external attributes is termed an **ego-protecting strategy**. All of us employ this self-serving attributional bias to maintain or improve our personal self-esteem. For this reason, ego-enhancing and ego-protecting strategies can maintain your self-confidence, and they can even be true at certain times. However, if you continue to use these self-serving attributions for almost every competitive outcome, you will only be fooling yourself in terms of what you need to do, or not do, to improve your performance.

NO EXCUSES

Carlos Beltran handled his tremendous disappointment with a dignity that was truly amazing. After taking a third strike to end the game and the New York Mets' World Series hopes on Thursday, October 19, 2006, Beltran offered no excuses and few regrets as he addressed one media group after another. He did not blame the home plate umpire, his teammates, the fans, the weather, or bad luck for his called third strike against St. Louis Cardinals closer Adam Wainwright. Instead, he focused on the positive aspects of the Mets' breakthrough season in the National League East. Beltran pointed out that his team had accomplished something very important —winning a division that had been owned by the Atlanta Braves for many years. In addition, he promised to approach next season with even greater resolve. Next year, he said, we're going to be a better ball club—we are going to get to the World Series. He also expressed complete faith that his team would accomplish that goal. Carlos Beltran epitomized how causal attributions can be used in a positive and proactive manner.

Highly skilled athletes tend to rely predominantly on internal factors to explain their performances

Athletes who have an internal locus of control usually believe it is their behaviors that influence performance outcomes. On the other side of the coin, athletes with an external locus of control usually attribute personal outcomes to external factors, such as other people (competitors) and good or bad luck. To elevate your performance over the long term, you need to believe you are in control of your own destiny. For example, if you honestly accept personal credit (internal factors) for a win or competitive success, this will not only improve your self-esteem but also increase your motivation for future contests.

THE BEST ATHLETES RELY ON INTERNAL ATTRIBUTIONS.

However, it is equally important that you learn to take responsibility for your own errors or lack of effort. Blaming others or other events (external factors) for your unsuccessful outcomes will prevent you from making the necessary adjustments to improve your future performances. If you continually blame something or someone other than yourself for a failure, you will have little motivation to improve your skills, your game strategy, or even the amount of effort you put out in any situation. It may even affect your relationship with your teammates. In the final analysis, there is really no doubt that internal attributions are your best strategy the majority of the time. So, remember to take responsibility for your own performances, and then make the necessary adjustments.

Highly skilled athletes view outcomes differently than do less-skilled athletes

It is interesting to note that elite, highly successful athletes do not evaluate their performances on the basis

Outcomes can be seen as positive if personal goals have been achieved.

of winning or losing alone. Rather, they tend to interpret their successes or failures on the basis of whether or not preestablished goals were met, or a self-assessment of their own personal effort and performance on that given day. For example, a top-notch team athlete will not feel responsible for a team loss if he or she performed at an optimal level. As long as personal goals were met, the outcome will be viewed as positive and successful. A baseball pitcher who throws a four-hitter and still loses the game 1-0 has nothing to be ashamed of. So go back and review Chapter 3, and focus strictly on achieving the performance and process goals you set for yourself.

Different attributions will cause you to feel different emotions

The attribution that you endorse after a successful or unsuccessful outcome will largely determine your resulting emotion or mood. When one of your successful outcomes is attributed to internal factors such as ability or effort, you will experience feelings of pride, satisfaction, competence, and increased confidence. But if you perceive an unsuccessful outcome to be the result of these same internal factors, you will probably feel ashamed, dissatisfied, incompetent, depressed,

ATTRIBUTIONS AND EMOTIONS ARE CLOSELY RELATED.

You may feel ashamed if you lose because of a lack of effort.

and less confident. It is therefore important to be proud when your successful performance is perceived as being caused by internal factors. But you also need to tough out those feelings of shame and dissatisfaction if your unsuccessful performance was perceived to be the result of your lack of effort or intensity on any given day.

If you attribute a successful outcome to external factors, such as luck or task (opponent) difficulty, you will likely feel grateful and thankful for your good fortune. You will realize that your positive outcome was not something you caused yourself, but you'll appreciate it nonetheless. On the other hand, if you perceive an unsuccessful outcome to be caused by these same external events, you will probably experience anger, astonishment, and even resentment. In either case, you need to focus on those factors that are within your personal control. So even if you attribute successful or unsuccessful outcomes to external factors, you need to continue striving for better preparation and 100% effort in every practice and contest. If you do this, you will continue to elevate your competitive performance.

Your attributions for success or failure can usually be predicted on the basis of others performing the same task

When the performance of other individuals or teams agrees with your own results, your attributions will likely be external. However, if the performance of others disagrees with your performance results, your attribution will probably be internal. For example, in a swimming heat, if you swim a faster time than an opponent who has beaten most other

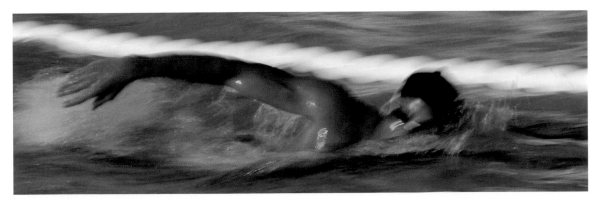

competitors, you will undoubtedly attribute your success to the internal attributions of ability or effort. Conversely, if you swim a faster time than a competitor who has lost to almost every swimmer, then you will likely attribute your success to the external attribute of that swimmer's lack of skill or conditioning (task difficulty). If you are competing against an inferior opponent, concentrate on the performance and process goals we talked about in Chapter 3. This will keep you focused on your performance and not on the competitors.

How Stability Attributions Affect You

Research also provides us with information about the implications of stability attributions for your personal success. Here we examine how your attributions will affect your expectancy for future success, and we show you how to avoid feelings of hopelessness when confronted with repeated unsuccessful outcomes.

Your expectancy for future competitions can be predicted by the attributions you endorse for present performances

Consider how you would feel if you had a long history of successful performances and then unexpectedly lost a competition. Similarly, consider how you would feel if you had a long history of unsuccessful performances and then unexpectedly won a competition. In either case, you will likely attribute your unexpected outcome to an unstable factor, such as luck, officiating, or even your personal effort. Research indicates that unstable attributions are usually given whenever an outcome is different from what you normally would have expected based on previous performances. On the other hand, stable attributions are usually offered when your outcome is what you would have expected based on past performances. This finding is important and once again suggests that you should make every attempt to attribute your unsuccessful performances to a lack of effort. If you endorse this unstable attribute, then you will readily recognize that greater effort on your part can easily turn that loss into a victory the next time you meet the same opponent.

If you have ever felt that events are out of control and failure is inevitable, then you are likely suffering from learned helplessness

Learned helplessness is probably a term you have not heard before. It is a psychological state in which you believe events and outcomes are completely beyond your control, resulting in a feeling of hopelessness. For example, it is highly likely that you have experienced a psychological "block" against facing certain opponents who have repeatedly beaten you in the past. This type of scenario usually develops because you have consistently attributed your lack of success to stable factors, such as lack of ability, in those past competitions. If you attribute failure or an unsuccessful outcome to a stable factor, it implies that failure is a realistic expectation for future encounters with that opponent or team. This process then becomes cyclical by causing you to feel demotivated in future meetings with that adversary. This demotivation then results in your putting out less effort to prepare for the next meeting, since you already subconsciously believe the outcome is inevitable. This will invariably result in another defeat.

To "short-circuit" this process, you need to focus on developing and maintaining your feelings of self-confidence and self-efficacy. Chapter 2 gives you a variety of tools to do just that, so go back and review that material carefully. In addition to following that important information, you need to concentrate on more important attributions for successful and unsuccessful outcomes. After successful performances, try to view the outcome as the result of the internal and stable attribute of ability. Taking credit for your accomplishments promotes pride, increases your self-confidence level, and leads you to expect success in future competitions. Conversely, after unsuccessful outcomes, make every effort to realize that the failure was likely the result of the unstable attribute of personal effort and preparation. If you constantly use these positive interpretations, you will understand that success is a very real possibility if you play with greater motivation and intensity in your next performance.

Learned helplessness results in big-time demotivation.

REMEMBER TO USE POSITIVE SELF-TALK.

Attributional Training for Optimal Performance

Now that you have learned the most important implications of the locus of control and stability attributions, it is time for you to learn how attributional training can have a positive impact on your athletic performance and expectations for future competitions. Attributional training usually consists of four basic steps. Each will now be outlined for your personal use.

Step 1 The first thing you need to do is record and classify the attributions you have made for past successful and unsuccessful performances. This can easily be done by honestly completing the causal attribution survey in Table 6.3 and by completing Personal Applications 6.1 and 6.2. But you need to repeat this process several times to reveal consistent attributional patterns you have endorsed.

STEP 1

Record and classify

STEP 2

Interpret and discuss

STEP 3

Resolve maladaptive attributions

STEP 4

Continually assess goals and attributions

Step 2 The next step involves taking a long and hard look at the attributions you identified in step 1. For example, if you notice that you have been consistently attributing unsuccessful outcomes to bad luck, bad officiating, or task (opponent) difficulty, it would be a good idea to discuss this finding with your coach. That way, you will get a second opinion to see if your coach agrees or disagrees with your interpretations. Your coach's viewpoint is likely to be more objective and should be carefully considered in your analysis.

Step 3 If step 2 indicates that your attributions match those of your coach, you do not need to make any immediate changes. But if your coach indicates that you have been consistently endorsing maladaptive attributions, then you need to work together to shift your focus to those all-important internal attributions over which you have complete control. You have already learned that successful sporting outcomes are invariably the result of stable and internal attributions, while unsuccessful efforts are usually caused by the unstable factor of personal effort. So concentrate on improving your own skill level, refining your game strategy, and maximizing your personal effort to get the best results.

Step 4 The last step is an ongoing process, and you need to follow it for the rest of your competitive career. Research indicates that the best attributional training results have occurred when athletes combine planned goal setting with attributional manipulation. Chapter 3 makes several recommendations for effective goal setting and outlines its overall value. In terms of attributional training, goal setting is very effective in helping you view success as a matter of reaching personal goals, rather than merely winning or losing an event. If you focus on achieving personal performance and process goals throughout the season, you will find it much easier to endorse the internal attributes of effort and ability. This will go a long way toward reducing your chances of making inappropriate attributions.

The following section provides a variety of suggestions to prevent, reduce, and even eliminate maladaptive attributions. By following these guidelines carefully, you will make the process of causal attribution work for you in your quest for optimal performance. You will also find that it greatly increases your motivation to improve over the long term.

A WELL-DEVELOPED GOAL-SETTING PLAN WILL HELP YOU INTERPRET OUTCOMES MORE APPROPRIATELY.

Making Causal Attributions Work for You

Now that you have learned all about the attribution process, it is time to examine how this important information can be put to work for your personal competitive advantage. You can motivate yourself to a higher level of performance by practicing the following easy-to-use strategies.

Be honest in your attributions
Your attributions must reflect reality; always remember to be totally honest in your interpretations. Although it is much easier to blame something or someone else for

your unsuccessful performances, a far better approach is to take responsibility for any given outcome. For example, if you come up flat in a game, just acknowledge that fact rather than blaming a referee, a teammate, or the weather for the result. Then go to work on preparing more adequately for the next competition.

Know when to use internal and external attributions Generally speaking, you should not use external attributions (luck or task difficulty) to explain your lack of goal achievement or your unsuccessful outcomes. This has the potential to promote the development of learned helplessness, since you continually view performance results as being out of your control. A far better approach is to focus on the internal attributes of skill development and effort. This way, you will spend your time productively, instead of lamenting events that were beyond your control. So as much as possible, rely on internal attributions for your performance outcomes. This will make you a better athlete and improve your motivation for future efforts.

Know when to use task difficulty attributions Sometimes, attributing failure to a difficult task can also be an effective strategy. Although this is not an internal attribute, there are times when it is the appropriate interpretation. Admitting that you lost to a better team or athlete today or saying that a particular opponent was unbeatable this time will maintain your confidence over the long haul. It will also prevent you from attributing the result to low ability on your part. As long as you honestly believe the task difficulty attribution is correct, it is a very effective technique for maintaining your competitive intensity.

Develop self-efficacy through meticulous preparation Few things are as important in competitive athletics as superior performance. Only when you have developed your physical and psychological skills to their maximum ability and you are totally prepared in game strategy will your self-efficacy be enhanced. This improved self-efficacy will go a long way toward promoting the most appropriate attributions. Superior preparation will also reduce potential feelings of learned helplessness and your tendency to go back to inappropriate external attributions. So the bottom line is that superior physical and mental skill preparation will lead to superior attributions, which in turn lead to even better skill development.

Task difficulty can prove to be a strong motivator.

Be positive when evaluating external factors Attributing your successful performances to luck ("I was lucky to win today") or an inferior opponent ("I only won today because my opponent performed poorly") is actually insulting to you as an athlete. Looking at these same two examples, a more appropriate comment involving the luck attribute might be "I caught a few good breaks and bounces today, but I played hard and deserved to win." A more effective task difficulty attribute would be "I competed against an excellent opponent today, but I still won—it's good to see how my hard work has paid off." Both these latter attributional statements will improve your self-confidence and motivate you to work harder and perform even better.

Personal Application 6.3 Developing personal attribution goals.

Using all the information provided in this chapter, set two personal goals outlining how you plan to use causal attributions in your future efforts. Be as specific as possible when stating the goals and the strategies you will use to meet them.

Goal #1: _____

Specific strategies: _____

_____

_____

Goal #2: _____

Specific strategies: _____

_____

_____

Summary and Conclusions

In this chapter, you learned that you will continually strive to understand the reasons for your successes and failures. Most of the time, you will likely rely on one of four attributional categories: ability, effort, task (opponent) difficulty, or luck. Of special relevance to you as an athlete is the fact that the particular attribute you endorse will go a long way toward determining your self-confidence, your resulting emotions, your motivation to improve, and your expectancy for success or failure in future competitive efforts. It is therefore very important to thoroughly analyze your personal attribution tendencies, then monitor them over the course of the season to make sure you are using them to your best advantage. This chapter gives you all the tools you need to accomplish this important task.

THE ATHLETE'S LIBRARY

Biddle, S.J. (1993). Attribution research and sport psychology. In R. Singer, M. Murphy, & L.K. Tennant (Eds.), *Handbook of research in sport psychology* (pp. 437-464). New York: Macmillan.

Biddle, S.J., & Hill, A.B. (1992). Attributions for objective outcome and subjective appraisal of performance: Their relationships with emotional reactions in sport. *British Journal of Social Psychology, 31,* 215-226.

Orbach, I., Singer, R., & Murphey, M. (1997). Changing attributions with an attribution training technique related to basketball dribbling. *The Sport Psychologist, 11,* 294-304.

Orbach, I., Singer, R., & Price, S. (1999). An attribution training program and achievement in sport. *The Sport Psychologist, 13,* 69-82.

KEY TERMS

attributional training

attribution scheme

causal attribution

ego-enhancing strategy

ego-protecting strategy

learned helplessness

locus of control attributions

open-ended measurement

perception

stability attributions

structural rating scale

CHAPTER CONTENTS

CHAPTER 7

SPECTATOR EFFECTS ON PERFORMANCE

OBJECTIVES

In this chapter you will learn:

❶ the concept of social facilitation theory

❷ the relationship between spectator presence and sport performance

❸ how spectator characteristics have the potential to improve or hinder your performance

❹ the advantages and disadvantages of an interactive audience

❺ specific guidelines that will improve your performance in front of an audience

The story below illustrates how sport is a social experience. Almost every athlete performs with teammates, competes against rivals, and interacts in one form or another with spectators. Sometimes the audience shows support by cheering, clapping, or holding up signs with positive messages. Other times they show disapproval by booing,

Brian was having a difficult time understanding how his performance could be fluctuating so much during his first year as a varsity quarterback. When his team played at home, he always seemed to be on top of his game, reading the defense accurately, finding primary and secondary receivers with precision, and selecting the perfect combination of passing and rushing options. During these home games, he felt completely in the zone. Although he played for a relatively small university, the fans were always supportive, and he felt completely comfortable every time he stepped on the field. Away games, however, painted a completely different picture. His pass-completion average was a full 20% lower in road games. To make matters worse, Brian found himself being indecisive in the huddles, calling conservative and predictable plays. The end result, of course, was that the opposing defense was shutting down Brian's offense with relative ease. Although Brian was aware of this, he couldn't seem to revert to the successful style he utilized at home. For some reason, he felt uncomfortable and distracted when he played on the road. When confronted with this problem by his coach, Brian was at a complete loss to explain why he played so well at home and so poorly when the team traveled to other universities.

whistling, jeering, shouting, or holding signs with insulting messages. Of all the social psychological phenomena in sport, few if any have as much of an impact on athletic performance as the audience. Sometimes this spectator effect is positive and performance is improved, and other times the effect is negative and performance drops off, as was the case with Brian in the opening scenario.

Few things can affect your performance more than an audience.

In this chapter, we will examine the nature of the relationship between spectators and performance, discuss relevant audience characteristics, and offer specific guidelines that will help you perform well in front of both friendly and unfriendly audiences. We begin with an overview of social facilitation theory.

Social Facilitation Theory

Spectators cause increased arousal in athletes.

The term social facilitation is often used to refer to the performance changes that occur because of the presence of others. Most athletes can readily identify with this concept. Think back to the times when you secretly wanted to perform better when your mother, father, significant other, or friends were present in the audience. This is only natural, since we all want to be perceived positively by the people who mean the most to us.

Social facilitation research has been influenced by drive theory, which suggests that the presence of an audience has the effect of increasing arousal in the performing athlete. Since an increase in arousal facilitates an occurrence of the dominant response, this means that performance can be either improved or hindered depending on the skill level and stage of learning. This relationship is illustrated in Figure 7.1.

Figure 7.1 Social facilitation as related to performance and learning.

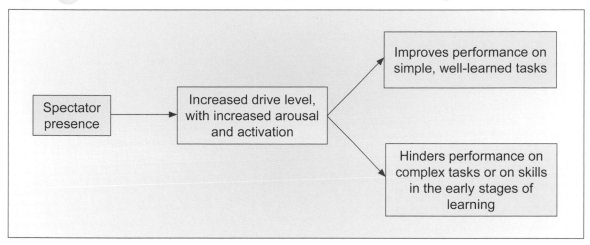

Later research takes this a step further, suggesting that a distinction must be made between whether or not the audience is important, relevant, or significant to the individual athlete. For example, spectators who are considered experts cause substantially more dominant responses than do spectators who are seen as nonexperts, or uninformed viewers. This highlights the importance of the evaluation component of spectator presence. It further points out that the "potential for evaluation" seems more important than the mere presence of spectators in raising or lowering drive level. Intuitively, this makes a great deal of sense.

Think of your own particular sport. If you were playing in an important contest, who would increase your drive level more—a group of professional athletes in your sport or a group of random spectators off the street? Obviously, you are going to try harder to impress the professionals, since you know they are experts in your sport and they can evaluate the intricacies of your performance. This increased drive level will in turn increase your arousal. This relationship is depicted in Figure 7.2.

Figure 7.2 Social facilitation as related to spectator expertise and evaluation potential.

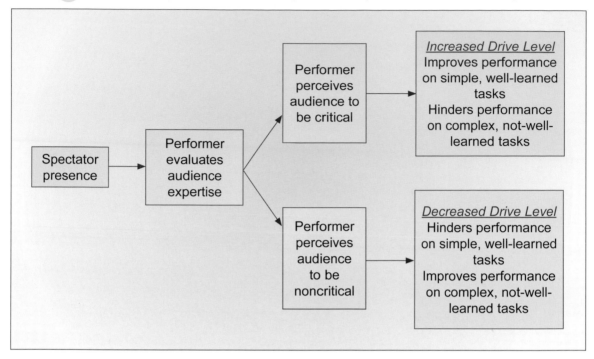

Much research has been conducted over the years in the area of spectator presence. For the most part, this research supports the drive theory perspective regarding the audience, arousal, and performance relationship. More recently, however, this position has come under closer scrutiny. It has been suggested that there is a fundamental flaw in the social facilitation research as it applies to competitive sport. As defined earlier in the chapter, social facilitation describes the performance changes that occur because of the presence of others. But "mere presence" seldom occurs in the world of competitive sport.

Athletes often interact in one form or another with the audience, and this involves much more than mere presence. For this reason, the remainder of this chapter will focus on research that addresses the interactive relationship between the athletes and the spectators. Before we do this, however, it is important for you to take a few minutes to consider how spectators affect you personally.

Personal Application 7.1 Identifying spectator characteristics that would affect your performance.

Pretend you are participating in a sporting event today that is very important to you as an individual. How do you think each of the following factors will affect your performance?

Audience Characteristic	Effect on Performance		Extent of Effect on Performance						
	Improve	Hinder	Low			Moderate			High
1. The audience is large.	_____	_____	1	2	3	4	5	6	7
2. The audience is small.	_____	_____	1	2	3	4	5	6	7
3. The audience is supportive.	_____	_____	1	2	3	4	5	6	7
4. The audience is not supportive.	_____	_____	1	2	3	4	5	6	7
5. People you don't know are present in the audience.	_____	_____	1	2	3	4	5	6	7
6. Friends are present in the audience.	_____	_____	1	2	3	4	5	6	7
7. Parents are present in the audience.	_____	_____	1	2	3	4	5	6	7
8. Your significant partner is present in the audience.	_____	_____	1	2	3	4	5	6	7
9. The audience is well informed about your sport.	_____	_____	1	2	3	4	5	6	7
10. The audience is not well informed about your sport.	_____	_____	1	2	3	4	5	6	7

Interactive Audience Effects on Performance

As mentioned previously, spectator "mere presence" rarely occurs in the world of competitive sport. Some type of interaction almost invariably occurs between the athlete(s) and the spectators. This interaction does not need to be verbal in nature, however; it can occur just by a heightened awareness that others are present. The psychological presence theory of audience arousal suggests that an athlete's arousal increases as the psychological presence of the

The more you allow spectators to "get in your head" the greater the chance they can hurt your performance.

audience/spectators increases. In other words, the more the spectators are "in your head," the more potential they have to distract you from your athletic performance.

One suggested reason for this is that psychologically present audiences cause more attentional conflict in the athlete by dividing that person's attention between the spectators and the task. If you have ever tried to study for an exam while listening to the radio, visiting with a friend, or watching TV, you will easily appreciate the concept of distraction theory. In Chapter 5, you learned the importance of maintaining attentional focus for achieving optimal sport performance. Think back to what you learned in that chapter, then take a few minutes to complete the following self-awareness exercise.

Personal Application 7.2 Regaining attentional focus with a psychologically present audience.

Looking back at the material presented in Chapter 5, explain how you could use the thought-stopping and centering intervention to regain your attentional focus when you become aware that the spectators are becoming distracting.

_____

_____

_____

_____

_____

_____

_____

_____

_____

_____

_____

_____

The Home Advantage

A home advantage has been proven to exist for certain sports.

A long-standing belief in organized sport is that home teams perform better than visiting teams. The relationship between an interactive audience and a home advantage has generated an extensive amount of research over the past 30 years. When one examines all the empirical research, it can reasonably be concluded that a home advantage exists for basketball, football, baseball, ice hockey, soccer, field hockey, alpine skiing, and cricket. In addition, a home country advantage exists relative to the Olympic Games. An extensive review of all studies investigating this phenomenon suggests that the advantage, although real, differs from sport to sport. For example, the greatest home advantage occurs in basketball, hockey, and soccer, while the smallest advantage occurs in baseball.

Although the home advantage is well documented, it is also possible that the home court/field can turn out to be a disadvantage, depending on the circumstances. Earlier in this chapter, you learned that spectators cause an increase in activation and arousal, and this increase in arousal can either improve or hinder your performance. So if you are playing in front of a very vocal and supportive audience, you could become overaroused and your performance would deteriorate, as suggested by drive theory.

The home advantage disappears if you lose focus and start to "press."

Another possibility for a home court/field disadvantage occurs if your fans place unreasonable expectations on you or your team to win. This could result in increased pressure, causing you to lose your attentional focus. Generally speaking, however, most experts agree that a home advantage exists in the majority of situations. Because there is little doubt that a home advantage occurs, recent researchers have shifted the focus of their attention to investigating specific audience characteristics in an attempt to determine the exact nature of this relationship.

Audience Characteristics and Home Advantage

Research has identified several factors that have potential to explain the home advantage, including crowd size, supportive home audiences, crowd density and intimacy, and disruptive away audiences. In addition, several nonaudience factors may be associated with the tendency for athletes and teams to perform better at home. Each of these will be briefly discussed in this section.

Crowd Size In baseball, the winning percentage of home teams has been found to increase as the size of the crowd increases. Although this is true, you will recall that hockey, basketball, and soccer seem to be the sports that experience the greatest home advantage. Traditionally, these three sports have a smaller number of spectators than do baseball or football. This suggests that although crowd size can improve performance, other crowd factors are more likely to be the cause of the home advantage. Two such factors are crowd intimacy and crowd density. Before we explain these terms, review your answers to questions 1 and 2 in Personal Application 7.1. What effect does crowd size have on you personally?

The Supportive Home Audience Many authors suggest that home advantage is the result of a supportive home audience. Most athletes can easily identify with the feeling of wanting to perform at the highest level when playing in front of a supportive and vocal audience. It is very motivating when the spectators clap, chant, and cheer for the home team. Obviously, the noisier the home audience, the more motivating it becomes. Some researchers suggest that baseball teams playing in domed stadiums have an advantage over teams playing in open-air stadiums because the domes hold in the noise, thereby providing a greater sense of support. Generally speaking, however, most athletes and teams benefit from a supportive home audience. Take a minute to review your answers to questions 3 and 4 in Personal Application 7.1. What effect do you believe a supportive audience has on you, and why do you think that is the case?

The noisier the home audience, the more motivating it becomes.

Crowd Intimacy and Crowd Density

Crowd intimacy and crowd density refer to how close the crowd is to the playing surface (intimacy) and how close the fans are to one another (density). In basketball and hockey, spectators are almost within arm's reach of the athletes. Soccer fans are somewhat farther from the field, but they are still relatively close compared with football or baseball. Along the same lines, basketball, hockey, and soccer fans are usually much more "tightly packed" into the seats, since the arenas and stadiums are somewhat smaller. This gives the appearance of a jam-packed stadium, so the crowds look bigger. Also, since the fans are closer to the playing surface and are seated more closely together, this has the effect of raising the noise level when the fans cheer, clap, or chant. This in turn gives the athletes the feeling that the crowd is even more supportive.

SPECTATORS THAT ARE "IN YOUR FACE" HAVE GREATER POTENTIAL TO AFFECT YOUR PERFORMANCE.

The Disruptive Away Audience

Another possible way to explain the home advantage is the disruptive away audience. While home audiences are usually supportive of the home team, they are often nonsupportive of the visiting team. This can take the form of booing, jeering, whistling, and shouting insults. A supportive home audience, then, can be hostile to the visiting team. Research indicates that sustained audience protests can actually improve the home team's performance while worsening the visiting team's performance. The only exception to this tendency is when the home audience becomes

abusive or antisocial. Examples include throwing objects on the court/field/ice, fighting, and verbal aggression (swearing at officials or players). When sustained audience protests become abusive, the result is usually a decrement in home team performance. Booing and whistling, however, are not considered antisocial acts and have the main effect of worsening the visiting team's performance.

LETTING THE FANS GET UNDER YOUR SKIN

On November 19, 2004, Indiana Pacer Ron Artest charged into the stands and fought with the fans in the final minute of a game against the Detroit Pistons. With less than a minute left in the contest, Artest was called for a flagrant foul on Detroit star Ben Wallace. This prompted Wallace to shove Artest forcefully with two hands, and Artest responded aggressively. Pacer and Piston players rushed the scene of the action, and this excited the fans, resulting in jeering and verbal abuse by the partisan Piston spectators. At one point, objects were thrown from the stands in Artest's direction. In response, Artest and his teammates rushed into the crowd, and punches were exchanged with the Detroit fans. The officials stopped the game with 45.9 seconds remaining, forcing an early and ugly end to the Pacers' 97–82 win. As a result of Artest's actions, he was suspended 73 games, the most in NBA history, and lost approximately $5 million in salary.

Other Nonaudience Factors Several nonaudience factors have been identified as possible reasons for the home advantage in sports. The most frequently cited of these include facility familiarity, travel fatigue, specific sports rules, and biased officiating.

Facility familiarity makes intuitive sense in that as athletes become more familiar with their home playing environments, their performances should improve. Notable examples include Fenway Park ("the Green Monster"), Yankee Stadium, Boston Gardens ("Celtic Mystique"), and the Montreal Forum. In each of these cases, the home team has enjoyed a good deal of success. Also, alpine skiers who train at a race venue have an advantage over competitors who may be skiing that course for the first time. Although the other skiers

Athletes become more familiar with their home playing environments.

may get three training runs, that still does not make them as familiar with the course as someone who trains there regularly. Similarly, both high school and university athletes feel more confident when they play at home. Although research does not confirm that facility familiarity is responsible for strong home team records, this notion persists with many coaches and athletes.

Travel fatigue is another nonaudience factor that has been suggested as contributing to home advantage. Jet lag, sleeping conditions, changes in diet, and changes in daily routine associated with extended travel all have potential to disrupt the visiting team's performance. Although this theory also makes a good deal of sense, research has not confirmed that travel fatigue is a determining factor in the home advantage.

Specific sports rules also appear to have the potential to cause a home advantage. For example, in baseball, the home team gets to bat last, and in ice hockey, the home team gets to make the last line change. At present, very little research has investigated this hypothesis, and what has been completed does not support the notion that specific sports rules are responsible for creating the home advantage. Much more research needs to be conducted on this particular theory.

Biased officiating is one nonaudience factor that has received some experimental support. Several studies have found that officials' calls tend to favor the home team. In the National Hockey League, for example, 18 out of 20 NHL referees awarded the home team more power play opportunities than the visiting team. It should be noted, however, that the officials' decisions may actually be an audience-related factor if their decision to award a penalty is influenced by the audience. Research is definitely needed to investigate this relationship further.

Team Quality and Home Advantage

Although we know that the home team wins more often than the visiting team, it is important to consider the effect of team quality on the home advantage. Research conducted in the NHL indicates

that although it is an advantage to play at home, the chances of winning are much greater for high-quality teams than for low-quality teams. Similar research investigating college basketball indicates that high-quality teams perform better at home than away, but low-quality teams experience the exact opposite effect—they perform better away than at home.

From these two research studies, investigating two different team sports, it appears that team quality is a moderating variable that determines the extent of the relationship between playing at home and the winning percentage. But either way, winning at home occurs much more often for high-quality teams than for low-quality teams. This is important information for the athlete, since team quality can be improved with effort, while many of the other audience and nonaudience factors remain out of the athlete's personal control.

Guidelines for Performing Well in Front of an Audience

Now that you have a good understanding of the audience, arousal, and performance relationship, it is important to recognize how you can use this theory to improve your personal sport performance. This section offers several recommendations that will help you use social facilitation theory to enhance your skill execution both at home and on the road. Spectators, unfamiliar competition environments, and changed daily routines may have a negative effect on your performance.

Accept the fact that spectators can affect your performance

A great deal of research has documented this fact, so there is no need to deny it for the sake of trying to appear unflappable. The key is to accept it and have a mental game plan in place so you can use the spectators to improve your performance and avoid any possible performance drop-off.

FOCUS ON WHAT YOU CAN CONTROL.

Focus on what you can control

In the previous section, you read that certain nonaudience characteristics, such as facility familiarity, specific sports rules, and biased officiating, have been used to explain the home advantage. All these factors are beyond your control, so there is no need to dwell on them. Instead, devote your attention and mental energy to specific actions you can take to use the audience effect to your personal advantage. The rest of these recommendations will help you do just that.

Devote a significant amount of time to "overlearning"

In other words, practice, practice, and practice some more. As you already learned, the increased arousal associated with a critical audience tends to result in improved performance on simple and well-learned skills but hindered performance on skills that are complex or not well learned. This makes it imperative that your skills are all well learned to the point of being automatic. Once a skill is mastered, it comes under automatic processing—the specific skill is still being monitored by the brain, but it requires little conscious attention because it is well learned. The best antidote to harmful audience effects is therefore skill mastery.

Team quality is a better predictor of outcome than is game location

Expanding on the previous point, the team's focus should always be on quality and execution of plays. When all athletes have mastered their specific skills, and the team has mastered the play book, the odds are very high that a winning performance will result regardless of where the game is being played. It is only when teams are of equal quality that the home team has the advantage.

When trying to perfect a new skill, it is wise to practice alone at the beginning After your coach demonstrates a new skill, spend time perfecting that skill in the absence of other people. Since the increased arousal associated with audience presence hinders the performance of skills that are not well learned, it is advantageous to practice alone until the skill becomes more automatic. Once that happens, the presence of spectators or teammates will not have a negative effect on your skill execution.

Develop an awareness of your own triggers and plan accordingly.

Get to know what audience characteristics affect you the most To get an appreciation of those audience characteristics that have the greatest potential to affect your performance, take the time to complete Personal Application 7.1. Knowledge is power, and once you have identified the situations that could cause you the most problems, you can then use the information in Chapter 2 to develop specific strategies for building and maintaining confidence in those situations.

Avoid "pressing" when playing in front of a supportive but expectant home audience Sometimes a home audience places very high or even unrealistic expectations on their team. This in turn usually leads to heightened self-attention, or self-awareness, in the performing athletes. When this happens, the athletes are in danger of becoming distracted and losing attentional focus. You learned all about this concept in Chapter 5. Because a performer is aware of the cost of not winning, he or she starts to "press," thereby negating the automatic execution of well-learned skills. When this happens to you, your skill level will invariably drop off. At this point, it is imperative that you use an intervention to regain your proper attentional focus.

Use thought stopping and centering to regain attentional control when experiencing negative audience effects Following from the preceding point, when you find yourself in danger of becoming distracted by either a hostile away audience or an overly expectant home audience, you need to use appropriate intervention strategies to refocus. Thought stopping and centering is outlined in Chapter 5 as one valuable technique to regain attentional control, and the use of this strategy is an absolute must. In addition, Chapter 2 highlights the importance of using positive self-talk to maintain confidence throughout your sporting contest. This intervention can prove to be very effective in dealing with the negative aspects of audience presence, and it will help you maintain your confidence once you have regained the proper attentional focus.

Thought stopping and centering can help you tune out an audience.

When playing away games, avoid changing your eating habits and daily routine Most top-caliber athletes follow a finely tuned routine on game day. They tend to go to bed and wake up at the same time, eat the same kinds of foods, use the same relaxation and visualization strategies, travel to the game site at precisely the same time, perform the same warm-up routine, and so on. You need to follow this same routine when you are playing away games. This will minimize the chances that you will experience nonaudience-effect performance drop-off when playing on the road.

Be proactive, not reactive, when playing on the road When playing away from home, you need to resist the urge to respond aggressively to the hostile audience. Avoid taking unnecessary penalties and fouls—this is exactly what the away audience wants you to do. In order not to put your team at a disadvantage, it is crucial that you focus on execution and stick to your original game plan. Learn to "feed off" the hostile audience, and focus this energy on more functionally assertive behavior. In other words, when the spectators start getting to you, turn it up a notch.

Summary and Conclusions

Learning to play well in front of both friendly and unfriendly audiences is absolutely essential in high-performance sports. It can reasonably be argued that you will never play in the absence of some form of audience, since at the very least your performance will be viewed by one or more competitors. At the other end of the continuum, you may someday find yourself competing in front of thousands of cheering or jeering spectators. It takes a special kind of skill to deal with this added pressure. In most cases, a supportive audience can enhance your performance, but in other cases it may actually have the opposite effect. In addition, hostile spectators have tremendous potential to distract you from your skill execution. But in both situations, you can control the nature of this audience effect.

To help you take advantage of this opportunity, this chapter exposes you to important research in the area of social facilitation theory. Audience presence has the effect of increasing drive level, and this can either improve or hinder your performance depending on how well learned or complex the skill is that you are trying to execute. Most athletes prefer to play at home and often enjoy more success there; many audience characteristics have been used to explain this home advantage. The chapter concludes with 10 specific guidelines for performing well in front of an audience. This section synthesizes the collective research and offers specific strategies for improving your performance and minimizing distraction in front of an audience.

THE ATHLETE'S LIBRARY

Agnew, G.A., & Carron, A.V. (1994). Crowd effects and the home advantage. *International Journal of Sport Psychology, 25,* 53-62.

Bray, S.R. (1999). The home advantage from an individual team perspective. *Journal of Applied Sport Psychology, 11,* 116-125.

Cox, R.H. (2002). *Sport psychology: Concepts and applications* (2nd ed.). Dubuque, IA: Brown.

Madrigal, R., & James, J. (1999). Team quality and the home advantage. *Journal of Sport Behavior, 22,* 381-398.

Wright, E.F., Voyer, D., Wright, R.D., & Roney, C. (1995). Supporting audiences and performance under pressure: The home-ice disadvantage in hockey championships. *Journal of Sport Behavior, 18,* 21-28.

KEY TERMS

crowd density	drive theory	psychological presence
crowd intimacy	evaluation component	social facilitation
crowd size	facility familiarity	supportive home audience
disruptive away audience	home advantage	

CHAPTER CONTENTS

CHAPTER 8

PREVENTING STALENESS AND BURNOUT DURING THE COMPETITIVE SEASON

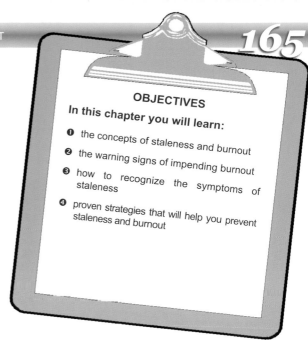

OBJECTIVES

In this chapter you will learn:

❶ the concepts of staleness and burnout

❷ the warning signs of impending burnout

❸ how to recognize the symptoms of staleness

❹ proven strategies that will help you prevent staleness and burnout

Situations like the one outlined in the box below are by no means uncommon in competitive sport. Sometimes the athlete takes drastic action and walks away from the sport for good, as Lori did. Other times, an athlete will stick with the sport, but unfortunately the downward spiral usually continues until some type of intervention is implemented, either by the coach or the athlete. These interventions have been proven to reverse the processes of staleness and burnout.

For the past six years, Lori had consistently been ranked among the top 10 female tennis players in the country. To date, her highest ranking was #5, achieved at the end of the previous season. Determined to elevate her standing, Lori had been training even harder than ever. She was playing more matches, traveling more, and utilizing all the traditional mental preparation strategies. Despite all this extra work, halfway through her new season, her ranking had slipped down to #8. This resulted in her doubling her practice time, watching more videos of past matches, and increasing the distance of her daily roadwork. To make matters even worse, despite her demanding training regimen, Lori was having trouble sleeping each night. Instead of getting her much-needed sleep, she found herself replaying in her mind the previous lost matches and agonizing over those defeats. Lori became more and more irritable with her family and friends with each passing day. Finally, midway through a practice session, Lori packed up her rackets, walked off the court, and left competitive tennis for good.

In this chapter, you will read about the symptoms and causes of burnout in athletics. More important from your perspective, you will learn how to recognize the problem at the outset and how to reduce or even prevent the occurrence of staleness or burnout in your competitive efforts.

Defining Staleness and Burnout

All athletes experience slumps from time to time.

Most athletes are more than familiar with the terms *slump*, *staleness*, and *burnout*. It is important for you to recognize what those terms have in common, as well as how they actually differ. This will allow you to recognize the warning signs and take action to stop the situation from deteriorating. Generally speaking, a slump is a specific performance-related phenomenon. If you have ever experienced prolonged periods when your performances have been poorer than usual, such as six games without a base hit, a ballooning number of unforced errors per tennis match, or a series of races where your times have been noticeably slower than usual, then you can bet your bottom dollar you have been experiencing a slump. It is interesting to realize that a slump may occur simultaneously with a period of staleness, or it *may be the result of that staleness*. Either way, the results are invariably the same—a series of poorer performances.

Staleness is a sign that burnout may not be far away.

The term staleness refers to an overall physical and emotional state. When this happens, you will begin to display a series of physiological and psychological symptoms that are the direct result of your previous performance drop-off. Most experts have defined staleness as a symptom of approaching burnout, or at the very least an early warning signal of worse things to come. If your staleness is not dealt with immediately and effectively, the odds are very high that you will soon experience athletic burnout.

This final stage, **burnout**, is described in the sport psychology literature as a state of mental, emotional, and physical exhaustion brought on by repeated unsuccessful attempts to meet the demands of your sport. If you continue to persist over a prolonged period of time in your quest to accomplish a goal that is not being achieved, you will almost invariably experience burnout. To determine if you are a candidate for burnout, ask yourself the following questions:

▶ Do I work much harder than other athletes in my sport?

▶ Do I work much longer in my practices and training sessions than other athletes?

▶ Do I train more intensely?

▶ Would my coach or teammates describe me as an overachiever?

▶ Do I consider myself to be a perfectionist?

▶ Would others define me as a perfectionist?

DO YOU SEE YOURSELF IN THESE QUESTIONS?

If you honestly answered "Yes" to several of these questions, then you may be susceptible to burnout. Research consistently shows that athletes who have problems with burnout are usually found to be dedicated perfectionists. Athletes with this profile tend to set goals that are unrealistic and then devote more time, energy, and intensity to achieve those goals than would be considered necessary under normal circumstances. The bottom line is that all this effort, persistence, time, and intensity can lead to physical and psychological exhaustion. If you think you are at risk, don't despair. In the remaining sections of this chapter, you will learn all about the causes and symptoms of staleness and burnout. This will allow you to recognize the problem before it gets out of hand. You will also be provided with a series of recommendations that can offset, or even prevent, the onset of staleness and burnout.

Understanding the Factors Leading to Burnout

The outcome of training stress can be positive or negative.

The whole idea of burnout is unfamiliar to recreational athletes. This is because recreational sporting pursuits differ greatly from competitive sports in terms of the necessary training and preparation requirements. In competitive sports, the main focus is to win, so both athletes and coaches devote much more time and intensity to training and practice activities. Athletes invariably practice daily, or several sessions daily, rather than weekly; the practices last longer; they are more demanding and exhausting; and the importance of every contest is greatly magnified. Much of the time, you probably feel as if you are in a pressure-cooker situation.

The end result of all this competitiveness is a significant increase in the amount of training stress you experience. Training stress can be viewed as a psychophysiological response to increased training. The outcome of training stress can be either positive or negative. A positive outcome is accompanied by a training gain. In this case, your performance improves as a result of the increased practice and training effort. Unfortunately, a negative outcome means no training gain. If this happens, you will see little or no improvement from the increased training. The natural tendency in this case is to train even harder. This

usually leads to overtraining, or a psychophysiological malfunction where you are actually training too hard. If you still do not see the desired improvements in your performance (i.e., a training gain), then it is highly likely that you will experience staleness. If you continue to experience this negative adaptation to training stress (no training gain) and staleness, you are well on your way to eventual burnout.

Recognizing Your Personal Symptoms of Burnout

IT IS CRUCIAL THAT YOU LEARN TO RECOGNIZE THE SYMPTOMS OF STALENESS.

It is important that you learn to recognize the early warning signs associated with staleness. By the time many of these symptoms are in full bloom, the problem will already be quite severe. For this reason, the best approach is to recognize the early signals, then take the appropriate action to prevent staleness from ever getting a firm foothold. This section of the chapter reviews what the research tells us about these early warning signals. Table 8.1 summarizes several physiological symptoms of staleness.

Table 8.1 Physiological symptoms of staleness in competitive sport.

- Higher resting and exercise heart rate
- Higher resting systolic blood pressure
- Delayed return to normal heart rate after exercise
- Increased muscle soreness and chronic muscle fatigue
- Elevated body temperature
- Weight loss
- Increased incidence of colds and respiratory infections
- Decreased maximum aerobic power
- Loss of appetite
- Decreased libido
- Subcostal aching (pain under the ribs)
- Bowel disorders

If several of these symptoms are occurring more often and lingering longer, talk to your coach.

The main problem with relying on physiological symptoms as an early personal warning system is that often they are very difficult to perceive accurately. For example, competitive sports invariably raise your heart rate and blood pressure, cause muscle fatigue, elevate your body temperature, and so on. You would have to be very "tuned in" to your bodily functions to notice the small differences that may be indicative of staleness. You also need to be completely honest with yourself in terms of what you are feeling. Athletes often tend to deny negative symptoms or explain them away as being the result of other lifestyle factors. For this reason, it is more beneficial for you to focus on psychological symptoms of staleness. Most of these symptoms are far easier to perceive and acknowledge.

Almost every athlete will experience one or more of these symptoms during the course of an athletic season. However, when you start noticing several of these psychological symptoms, and they are lasting for a prolonged period of time, it usually suggests you are experiencing staleness. It is absolutely necessary that you talk to the coach about your concerns. He or she will be able to help you get back on track. To determine if you are a candidate for staleness, complete Personal Application 8.1.

Personal Application 8.1 Identifying psychological symptoms associated with staleness.

Over the next several games and practices, use this checklist to determine if you are a candidate for staleness. Honestly consider the following questions, then place a checkmark beside those that apply to you.

1. Have I been experiencing a lack of self-confidence lately?   _____

2. Have I been feeling excessive weariness that is prolonged?   _____

3. Are my interactions with teammates deteriorating?   _____

4. Do I feel generally apathetic or lack my normal feelings?   _____

5. Am I more irritable than usual?   _____

6. Have I been experiencing more moodiness than usual?   _____

7. Am I feeling more depressed than usual?   _____

8. Do I feel more anxious or nervous than usual?   _____

9. Have I been experiencing periods when I feel more confused?   _____

10. Have I been displaying more anger or hostility than usual?   _____

Discuss your feelings and concerns with your coach.

If you have checked several of these items, talk to your coach about the feelings you are experiencing. In fact, your coach or teammates have probably already noticed some of these symptoms. Usually, the coach will be able to make some recommendations and adjustments that can reverse the negative trend. In extreme cases, however, where you are consistently exhibiting most of these psychological symptoms, simultaneously and at high levels of intensity, your coach may refer you to a certified counselor or sport psychologist. Either of these professionals can help you determine the root of the problem and can get you back to your original level of sport enjoyment and fulfillment.

What Causes Staleness in Competitive Sport?

Before you can start developing a plan for preventing personal staleness, it is first necessary to understand how this whole process is associated with training and competition. Research suggests that a variety of factors contribute to this problem. The most common of these are listed in Table 8.2.

Table 8.2 Common causes of staleness in competitive sport.

- Length of the competitive season
- Perceived monotony of daily training
- General boredom
- Lack of positive reinforcement
- Excessively stringent rules
- Feelings of claustrophobia
- Perceived low accomplishment
- Perceived training overload
- High levels of competitive stress
- Feelings of helplessness
- Abuse from coaches and other authority figures

MANY FACTORS CONTRIBUTE TO STALENESS IN SPORT.

Length of season is a major contributor to staleness.

Most research experts agree that the single most significant contributor to athletic staleness is the length of the season. In today's world of highly competitive sports, many athletes have seasons that run virtually year-round. Although competitive sport seasons usually have a specified length, most athletes feel the need to continue their training regimens all year. This is an easy trap to fall into indeed, since you probably believe that if you take some time off, your competitors will be gaining on you. Although this may be true in the short term, over the long haul you will be far better off if you schedule some downtime or time-outs over the course of the year. These breaks allow you to "recharge" your batteries and also reduce your chances of encountering staleness problems.

Closely related to the previous point, prolonged training invariably leads to a feeling of monotony. When this happens, you will become bored with your training efforts and probably not put out the same level of intensity that you did when the season started.

Many athletes make the mistake of assuming a "more is better" philosophy. If two hours of practice a week is good, then four is better, and eight is better still. But in actual fact, exercise science research has found that a complete linear relationship between increased training and improved strength, endurance, and performance simply does not exist. In other words, more is not always better. Many wise coaches would probably suggest that fewer training hours are needed *if practice and training sessions are of a higher level of intensity and quality*. So rather than continuing the spiral to more and more hours, concentrate on making every minute of every training session count.

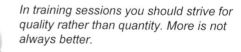

In training sessions you should strive for quality rather than quantity. More is not always better.

EVEN THE BEST CAN BECOME STALE

On October 6, 1993, Michael Jordan announced his retirement from professional basketball, citing a lost desire to play the game. On an Oprah Winfrey show, he commented that opposing defenses had "taken away his air." Jordan also stated that he had reached all his personal basketball goals and no longer wished to compete. However, on March 18, 1995, he announced his comeback to the NBA with a two-word press release: "I'm back." He retired for a second time on January 13, 1999, only to announce his return to action less than three years later on September 25, 2001. Jordan's last professional game was April 16, 2003, against the Philadelphia 76ers. In that game, he sank his last two free throws, then exited to a standing ovation. Jordan's final retirement left him with 32,292 career points, placing him third on the all-time scoring list behind Kareem Abdul-Jabbar and Karl Malone.

Finally, you have probably noticed from Table 8.2 that several environmental factors can combine to precipitate the onset of staleness. For example, if you experience repeated abusive comments from your coach, receive little or no positive reinforcement, and participate in a team atmosphere with excessively strict rules, then you are a candidate for staleness and eventual burnout. You will perceive all these factors as coming together to create a feeling that things are "completely out of control." When this happens, you will begin to feel trapped in a hopeless situation, creating the general feeling of claustrophobia. This in turn leads to just "going through the motions" in both games and practices.

When all these factors are combined with the extremely high levels of competitive stress, you find yourself in a no-win situation. Because most athletes do not have the knowledge, training, and experience to handle problems of this nature, staleness is frequently the final outcome. This brings us to the most important section of this chapter. What can be done to prevent staleness and burnout? How can you head off the problem before it begins to occur? And,

Personal Application 8.2 A retrospective analysis of your sporting experiences.

As a self-awareness exercise, take a few moments to think back on your sporting career. Have you ever found yourself in a prolonged slump? Taking this a step further, can you recall instances when you have experienced the signs and symptoms of staleness? What were those signs and symptoms? Knowing what you know now about the possible causes of staleness in athletics, have there been times when you may have inadvertently contributed to the problem? How would you react differently if you could go back in time and do it all over again?

In my sporting career I recall the following prolonged slumps:

_____

_____

_____

_____

I experienced the following signs of staleness:

_____

_____

_____

_____

My reactions to the signs of staleness were:

_____

_____

_____

_____

Today I would react differently to the signs of staleness:

_____

_____

_____

_____

if early signs of staleness are evident, what can you do to reverse the situation? The following section offers a series of suggestions and recommendations that you can employ yourself to prevent the problem of staleness and possible burnout in your sport of choice.

Techniques to Help You Avoid Staleness and Burnout

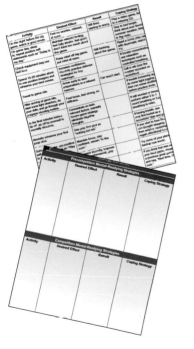

Research conducted in psychology, organizational behavior, and sport psychology has provided us with several recommendations that have excellent potential for preventing personal staleness and burnout. Each of these will now be summarized for your consideration and future use.

Develop a plan for prevention

The best way to prevent staleness and burnout is to have a specific plan in place that will head off the problem before it can get a foothold. You have already learned one very important thing to avoid: excessive training, or training that continues to increase in both time and intensity without demonstrating any observable improvements. Remember the suggestion in the previous section to maximize the *quality* rather than the *quantity* of your practice sessions. One of the easiest ways to do this is to have a well-developed series of personal practice sessions in place before the season even starts. Your coach can help you design these off-season practices.

In Chapter 3, you were provided with the information to help you develop both precompetition and competition strategy worksheets. You will recall that these worksheets allow you to put together a yearly training plan. The main advantage of the yearly training program is that it provides you with a working blueprint for your personal athletic development throughout the entire year.

One of the major goals of all-year training is ensuring the proper personal pace of conditioning and skill development. The most

Have a well-developed plan for practice sessions and precompetition and competition strategies.

effective plan is one that builds on your successful accomplishment of previously established goals. As well as outlining technical and conditioning goals, training plans also include the very important aspect of mental training. You have already learned the many benefits of mental training on both skill development and stress management. So remember to take the time before the season even begins to formulate a yearly training program that will ensure the proper planning and pacing of your training efforts.

It is a good idea to work directly with your coach to develop your personal yearly training plan, since he or she will also have training goals in mind for you and other team members. By working together, you and your coach can mesh your respective plans in a way that will maximize your sporting potential and hopefully prevent staleness and burnout from occurring over the course of your athletic season.

Keep the season's length in proper perspective

Length of the season may just be the single most significant factor in causing athletic staleness and burnout. Although the official length of the sport season is determined by high school activity associations and national sport governing bodies (including colleges and universities), many coaches and institutions encourage illegal training time. This is done by scheduling practice and training sessions outside the legislated guidelines. In the world of highly competitive sport, it is understandable that this could happen. It all comes down to the "more is better" philosophy we discussed earlier.

Control your pace and focus during a long season.

Both coaches and athletes believe that more training and more practice sessions are the last piece of the puzzle in achieving sports excellence and winning championships. But remember, a sport season is more of a marathon than a sprint. If you start too fast and fail to control your pace over the whole race, you will invariably "hit the wall." This is exactly what happens when staleness and burnout occur. So keep your focus directed on the big picture at the end of the season, and continue to tell yourself that to eventually win, you need to stay in the game. Pace yourself accordingly.

If you plan time-outs you can become more effective and reach higher levels of performance.

Be creative in scheduling planned time-outs

It is essential for your mental wellness that you experience periods of downtime, or time away from the stress of practices and competitions. As an athlete, you are no different from the millions of people who have to work for a living. Most business organizations recognize the importance of scheduled time-outs for their workers. This is why they provide vacation time, professional development days, statutory holidays, and even weekends away from the working environment. This is not done just out of the goodness of their hearts, but rather because research has repeatedly shown that workers are more productive and effective in the long term if they receive this valuable downtime.

Unfortunately, many athletes and coaches believe that taking a break is a sign of weakness or lack of motivation. In reality, nothing could be further from the truth. Any time-out used appropriately will cause you to feel more refreshed and invigorated. This in turn will increase your intensity upon return and ultimately lead you to a higher level of performance. And yes, it has the added bonus of keeping staleness and burnout from preventing you from reaching your athletic goals.

REWARD YOURSELF BOTH PHYSICALLY AND MENTALLY.

Reward yourself constantly

By now, you have a good idea of the value of positive reinforcement. In Chapter 2, you learned all about using positive self-statements to build and maintain personal self-confidence. In the best of worlds, your parents, coach, teammates, and fans will shower you with all the recognition you deserve. But in reality, these individuals have other things on their minds besides your progress. For this reason, it is a far better idea to use reinforcing self-statements during competitions, during practices, and even at home. Don't be afraid to tell yourself, "Great practice today—you really put out," or "That was the best defense you have played this year—great effort." You may want to refer to Chapter 2 and Chapter 3 to refresh your memory about how to use appropriate self-statements and avoid negative thoughts.

SUPER EFFORT! GREAT PRACTICE!

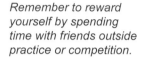

Remember to reward yourself by spending time with friends outside practice or competition.

Finally, don't forget to physically reward yourself from time to time. After a stellar performance or a great week of practice and training, treat yourself to a night out with your friends. Take in a good show or enjoy a pizza with someone you care about. You did great, so enjoy the moment. Remember, low self-confidence has been identified as an underlying symptom of staleness. Fortunately, the use of positive self-statements greatly decreases the likelihood that you will perceive low levels of accomplishment, another stated cause of staleness. So remember, positively reinforce yourself on a regular basis. This will greatly diminish your chances of coming face to face with staleness or eventual burnout.

Include mental practice periods in your training sessions

Another way to prevent staleness is to add variety to your training regimen. This has been proven very effective for increasing your motivation and maintaining your focus over the course of a season. One of the best ways to add variety is to incorporate periods of mental training within your usual physical training sessions. In Chapter 3, you saw how this concept can be included in a yearly training program, as well as in individual practice sessions. This technique not only breaks up the monotony of your practices but also provides your body with a much-needed physical break from the rigors of your training session. Many experts (and athletes) have found breathing and relaxation exercises, followed by sessions of positive imagery and mental rehearsal, to be highly effective in this regard. These brief mental training sessions will improve your self-confidence, give your performance a much-needed boost, and allow you to return refreshed and ready to go for the remainder of the training session.

Mental practice periods can provide a nice break from physical practice.

BE PROACTIVE IN YOUR GOAL SETTING.

Take some control over your choices and outcomes

Actively participate in some aspects of the decision-making process, such as designing your training schedule or discussing viable downtimes. Becoming actively involved in the group goal-setting process is another way to take some control over your personal training. Many athletes often just sit back and wait for the goal-setting session to be over. A far better approach is to become involved in these discussions and voice your opinions and suggestions when solicited. You may want to refer to Chapter 3 and examine once again the details and suggestions regarding goal setting for maximum performance.

Active participation will give you the feeling of exercising some personal control in the sport of your choice. Most coaches are more than happy to allow for this type of input and feedback. They know that getting the athletes involved in some aspects of the decision-making process actually increases motivation and perseverance during the tedium of regular practice sessions. Another suggestion is to talk to your coach about the possibility of self-planned workouts to supplement those designed by the coach himself or herself. Obviously, there are many more possibilities you may wish to consider. The main point to remember is that the feeling of having no control is a primary contributor to the occurrence of personal staleness and eventual burnout. So get involved with your own destiny, and you will quickly see that you are taking an important step to decrease the likelihood of staleness and burnout occurring during your competitive season, and maybe even your entire sporting career. This will be time well spent.

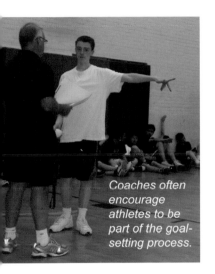

Coaches often encourage athletes to be part of the goal-setting process.

Actively monitor and manage both precompetitive and postcompetitive stress

Chapter 4 describes several specific techniques that have the potential to help you control your precompetitive stress and anxiety. Even before reading this book, you probably developed some "tried and true" strategies to keep your nervousness at bay before the start of a big competition. Now you have an even larger arsenal to stave off those precompetition jitters. But the process does not stop there. A workable strategy for handling your

postcompetition anxiety is necessary as well. Research consistently shows that athletes who remain constantly frustrated, resentful, and anxious before or after competition will eventually experience staleness and burnout.

The relationship between postcompetitive stress and staleness/burnout is a relatively recent area of sport psychological research. However, several important recommendations have emerged from the early research that will prove useful in your personal attempts to manage postcompetitive stress. By following these guidelines, you will significantly reduce the chances of experiencing staleness and burnout. The following suggestions should go a long way toward helping you handle the nagging postcompetitive stress that often accompanies competitive sport:

REMEMBER TO LISTEN TO YOUR BODY.

▶ Talk with your teammates while you are showering and dressing. Don't just sit there and mope.

▶ Always be supportive of your teammates. Remember, they are probably feeling the same emotions you are. By providing a willing ear and a kind word, you will be helping not only your friends but also yourself by taking your mind off your own feelings.

▶ The previous suggestion requires you to remain with your teammates as much as possible immediately after the contest. Leave the interviews until later, and by no means "run off" to sulk or hide. This will only exacerbate the problem.

A debriefing session is helpful after a competition.

▶ Related to the previous point, it is a good idea to stay away from well-meaning parents and friends until you have had a chance to "debrief" yourself on your feelings and the causes of those feelings. In a postcompetition setting, conversations of this nature tend to escalate your feelings of anxiety and lead to even more stress.

▶ Start to develop, in your own mind, an unemotional yet realistic appraisal of your personal performance during the recent competition. What did you do well? What could you have done better? How will you approach the next contest?

▶ Never, never let yourself gloat over a success or be overly depressed by a loss. There is always another day and "new fish to fry."

▶ Focus on "getting on with the program," and start preparing both physically and mentally for your next opponent. Today's contest is over and beyond your control. The next one isn't!

▶ If at all possible, get together with the team, or a smaller group of closer friends on the team, to discuss openly and honestly what transpired during the competition—a catharsis of sorts. Don't be afraid to share your feelings or concerns. Your friends are waiting to do the same.

▶ Listen to your coach. He or she will be able to provide a more objective and realistic postgame analysis than you. He or she can also offer a variety of workable techniques to handle the problematic postcompetitive stress you are experiencing.

If you follow these guidelines, you will be on your way to personally handling, in an effective manner, the negative feelings that often result from a competitive performance. This in turn will greatly decrease your chances of becoming stale or eventually reaching the burnout stage.

Summary and Conclusions

In this chapter, you learned that staleness and burnout are very real physiological and psychological problems that can crop up during the athletic season. No matter how excellent you are as an athlete, all your skills and years of meticulous preparation will be of little value if you encounter staleness or ultimate burnout. One of the early effects on your performance will be prolonged periods of substandard play, known as slumps. These slumps are very stressful for any competitive athlete because your position on the team is ultimately determined by day-to-day performance. In this chapter, you learned the major factors that cause staleness or burnout and how to recognize the early warning signals. Perhaps most important for you personally are the guidelines, or techniques, to help you stave off this serious situation.

Review the information, then complete Personal Application 8.3. If you follow the goals you set, your chances of encountering staleness and burnout will be greatly diminished.

Personal Application 8.3 Putting the research to work for you.

Using all the information provided in this chapter, outline the specific steps you are going to take to reduce your chances of experiencing staleness or burnout in your sport. Remember to be as specific as possible in outlining your strategies. If you need to refresh your memory on effective goal setting, refer to the guidelines offered in Chapter 3.

1. _____
   _____
   _____

2. _____
   _____
   _____

3. _____
   _____
   _____

4. _____
   _____
   _____

5. _____
   _____
   _____

6. _____
   _____
   _____

THE ATHLETE'S LIBRARY

Cherniss, G. (1995). *Beyond burnout*. London: Routledge.

Coakley, J. (1992). Burnout among adolescents: A personal failure or a social problem? *Social Psychology of Sport Journal, 9*, 271-285.

Gould, D., Udry, E., Tuffey, S., & Loehr, J. (1996). Burnout in competitive junior tennis players: A qualitative psychological assessment. *The Sport Psychologist, 10*, 322-340.

Henschen, K. (1999). Maladaptive fatigue syndrome and emotions in sport. In Y.L. Harris (Ed.), *Emotions in sport* (pp. 231-242). Champaign, IL: Human Kinetics.

Kuipers, H. (1996). How much is too much? Performance aspects of overtraining. *Research Quarterly for Exercise and Sport, 67*(Suppl. 3), 65-69.

Silva, J.M. (1990). An analysis of the training stress syndrome in competitive athletics. *Journal of Applied Sport Psychology, 2*, 5-20.

KEY TERMS

burnout

excessive training

illegal training time

overtraining

pace of conditioning

postcompetition anxiety

slump

staleness

training gain

training stress

CHAPTER CONTENTS

CHAPTER 9

IS THERE LIFE AFTER SPORT? TRANSITION ISSUES FOR ATHLETES

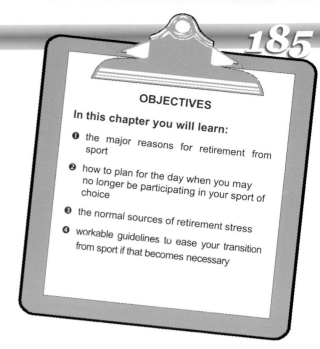

OBJECTIVES

In this chapter you will learn:

❶ the major reasons for retirement from sport

❷ how to plan for the day when you may no longer be participating in your sport of choice

❸ the normal sources of retirement stress

❹ workable guidelines to ease your transition from sport if that becomes necessary

The feelings Tim describes below are very common after leaving a longtime sport. Most athletes will experience a strong sense of loss when they leave competitive athletics. This is often accompanied by a loss of confidence, self-worth, perceived competence, and status. Athletes often report the feeling that retirement from sport has changed them from a "somebody" to a "nobody." All these factors

Although Tim had thoroughly enjoyed his five years of varsity football at a major university, he was secretly looking forward to having some serious downtime once his playing days were behind him. After playing football all through high school and university, he thought it would be fun to try some different things and explore some new hobbies. After his last game, he said to his closest teammate, "From here on, I am in complete control of my own life—no more practices, workouts, or road games." It came as a complete surprise to Tim that things did not turn out at all like planned. Although he did enjoy the feeling of more personal control, he also felt somewhat "lost" and isolated. Over the years, Tim had enjoyed the feeling that other students looked up to him as a star varsity athlete. He always felt like a "somebody" on campus. Now, he had graduated from university, the team had disbanded, and he no longer was able to hang out with his friends on the team. All of a sudden, Tim had become a regular guy. And although many new opportunities beckoned, it just seemed like too much work to get involved in other pursuits. Tim's normally upbeat mood disappeared, leaving him feeling strangely sad and anxious. He wondered secretly what he could have done differently to make his exit from sport easier. It wasn't supposed to be like this.

RETIREMENT FROM SPORT CAN BE TRAUMATIC.

combine to create a feeling of apprehension and uncertainty about the future, often resulting in significant distress and even depression. In this chapter, you will learn about the problems associated with retirement from sport and will be provided with a series of strategies that will make your personal transition from sport as easy as possible.

Reasons for Retirement from Sport

The most common reasons for ending an athletic career are associated with four factors: age, injury, free choice, and deselection. Each of these will now be examined in more detail.

Age

Research indicates that the decline in performance associated with advancing age is a primary cause of retirement. This relationship between age and career termination is likely the result of physio-

Martina Navratilova's professional tennis career spanned four decades. She retired in 2006, just prior to her 50th birthday.

logical, psychological, and social factors. In most sports, athletes can compete successfully into their 30s, or even their 40s. Notable sport examples include hockey, golf, and baseball. At some point in time, however, the natural deterioration associated with aging (strength, flexibility, reflexes, and so on) will result in diminished athletic performance. At the other end of the continuum, in elite sports where best performances most often occur during adolescence, athletes may retire from sport when they are still teenagers. A common example of this is women's gymnastics. In this sport, the onset of puberty and the accompanying physical changes associated with the growth spurt actually inhibit athletic performance.

Age also has a psychological influence on the decision to leave sport. In many cases, when ath-

Age is the primary cause of retirement.

letes become older, they lose their motivation to continue participating. In addition, highly successful athletes sometimes conclude that they have already reached their competitive goals and see no reason to continue. Notable examples include Bjorn Borg (tennis) and Michael Jordan (basketball). Finally, age also involves a social element. Fans, teammates, management, and even the media tend to devalue the "aging" athlete. This loss of perceived status can be the final straw in the decision to retire from sport.

WHAT CAN YOU DO AFTER A CAREER LIKE THIS?

On Sunday, September 3, 2006, Andre Agassi's illustrious career came to a tearful end. Losing 7-5, 6-7 (7-4), 6-4, 7-5 to Benjamin Becker in the third round of the U.S. Open, Agassi sat in the locker room and wrestled with conflicting emotions. On the one hand, there was the concrete knowledge that his historic tennis career had finally come to a close. But there was also the freeing sense of excitement that he would have more time on his hands to devote to his wife, Steffi Graf, and their two children, as well as to pursue other interests. Agassi's retirement from professional tennis will undoubtedly be a difficult transition because he has done it all in professional sport. The following represents a summary of his most notable accomplishments:

Turned pro: 1986
Career singles titles: 60
Grand Slam singles titles: 8
Career record: 870-274
Career Grand Slam record: 224-53
Career prize money: US$31,152,975

Injury

According to the research, up to one-third of all athletes retire prematurely because of a serious injury. In addition, severe injuries have been associated with a variety of psychological problems, such as loss of self-esteem, depression, anxiety, and even substance abuse.

ONE OUT OF EVERY THREE ATHLETES RETIRES BECAUSE OF INJURY.

In fact, some research indicates that athletes who retire due to injury have a more difficult transition from sport than those athletes who had the luxury of greater control over when their careers ended. Injury can also have the effect of limiting athletes in terms of their choice of new activities, and even their choice of careers.

Quarterback Joe Theismann's career was ended because of a horrific leg injury suffered during a game.

Free Choice

If you are going to retire from sport, free choice is the least stressful option.

Another common reason for retirement among elite and amateur athletes is simply the free choice of the athlete. This is the most desirable of reasons for leaving sport, since the decision resides completely within the control of the athlete. An athlete may choose to end his or her sport career for a variety of personal, social, and sport-related reasons. For example, an athlete may want to engage in new challenges or may experience a change in values and motivations. Other times, athletes in career transition have decided to leave sport to spend more time with their families and friends or to discover new social circles.

Finally, sometimes athletes leave competition because they have reached all their sport-related goals, leaving continued participation unenjoyable and unrewarding. It is interesting to note, however, that just because an athlete retires from sport voluntarily does not mean that he or she will not experience transition difficulties. Sometimes this voluntary decision is in response to a negative situation, such as conflict with a coach or the continual high stress of competition.

Deselection

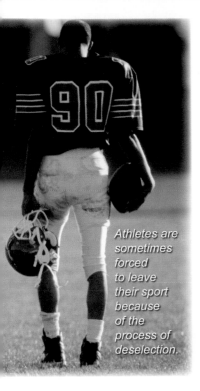

Athletes are sometimes forced to leave their sport because of the process of deselection.

The nature of the selection process that occurs at every level of competitive sport is another frequent reason for career termination. Because winning still remains the top priority in sports at all levels of competition, this process selects only those athletes who have the greatest potential for helping the team win. This same process "weeds out" those who are performing at a lower level, deselecting them from the team. This Darwinian "survival of the fittest" attitude is responsible for many athletes leaving their sport of choice involuntarily.

Possible Areas of Retirement Stress

When an athlete retires from sport, he or she is often faced with a wide range of psychological, social, financial, and vocational changes. The extent of these changes, and the athlete's perception of them, often predict the quality of the transition from sport. In this section, we examine some of the most common sources of retirement stress.

Self-Identity

One of the most fundamental problems associated with career transition is the fact that athletes often define their sense of self-worth in terms of their participation and achievement in sports. Because most elite athletes have been intensely immersed in their sports to the exclusion of other activities, they tend to have a self-identity that

Athletes often define their self-worth in terms of sports achievement.

is almost exclusively based on their sport involvement. This narrow self-identity becomes problematic once an athlete retires from his or her sport. Without continued sport involvement, retired athletes have little to support their sense of self-worth.

Research indicates that athletes who define their self-identity in terms of sport involvement are less prepared for careers after sport, have limited career and educational plans, and tend to view retirement from sport as a significant loss of something important that can never be recovered. The bottom line is that athletes who have overly defined their identity in terms of sport participation tend to experience the most transition stress.

Personal Application 9.1 How do you define your self-identity?

Take a few minutes to think about how you would define yourself as a person. What are your strongest attributes? It might be easier for you to complete this exercise by answering the following question: "My closest friends would describe me as . . ."

➢ _____

_____

_____

➢ _____

_____

_____

➢ _____

_____

_____

➢ _____

_____

_____

Social Identity

Elite and professional athletes enjoy a good degree of fame and social recognition. For this reason, many athletes define themselves in terms of the recognition and popularity that have resulted from their sport careers. In addition, most athletes do most of their socializing with other athletes in the sporting environment. This results in **role restriction**. In other words, since athletes often learn to assume certain social roles that are specific to the sport setting, their ability to assume other roles after retirement from sport may be severely limited.

Research consistently shows that those athletes with a broad-based **role identity** that includes family, friends, and educational and career components invariably experience an easier transition when it comes time to retire from sport participation.

Some retired athletes continue in their sport of choice in another capacity. Former NHL goaltender Kelly Hrudey now works as an analyst for Hockey Night in Canada.

Perception of Personal Control

Generally speaking, an elite athlete has very little control over his or her life. One very important issue regarding perceived control in career transition is whether athletes leave their sport by free choice or are forced to retire. The amount of perceived control in the decision to leave sport will greatly affect the transition process.

Loss of control is often associated with feelings of helplessness, depression, and anxiety.

Research from the field of psychology indicates that perceptions of control are closely related to feelings of self-competence and self-worth. In addition, the perception of loss of control is associated with feelings of helplessness, depression, and anxiety. This means that of the four causes of sport retirement—age, injury, free choice, and deselection—only free choice involves personal control. The absence of control over an event that is so intimately connected to an athlete's sense of self-identity and self-worth may create a highly emotional and threatening situation. Later in this chapter, you will be given several strategies to help prevent and alleviate the negative feelings associated with the perception of loss of personal control.

Other Possible Sources of Retirement Stress

In addition to the perception of control issue just mentioned, when an athlete retires from sport, he or she has a great deal more independence than was the case while competing. Elite and professional athletes have most of their decisions made for them by the coach or trainer while competing, so once they retire from sport, it becomes necessary to learn to make their own decisions. Although this is a welcome situation for most athletes, it does take a bit of time to adjust to the new independence, and change often involves a certain amount of stress.

Another possible source of stress relates to uncertainty about the future. While competing, many athletes often ignore the fact that sport is a short-lived career. Unless the athlete has planned accordingly, he or she may not have the necessary skills or training for a postsport career. For many professional athletes, education is often sacrificed in pursuit of sport excellence. After retiring from sport, these individuals find themselves in the stressful position of not having adequate skills or training for a new career.

Finally, professional athletes will usually experience a decrease in income upon retiring. Unless they have invested their money wisely, it may become necessary to make some significant changes to their style of living. Many people spend to a level commensurate with their earnings, so it is only natural to experience distress with reduced income.

Without proper planning, some retired athletes can't afford what they once enjoyed.

Recommended Strategies to Ease the Transition from Sport

Certain factors have been found to characterize smooth, problem-free retirements from sport. Athletes who have many of these factors working in their favor can usually experience an easier transition. These common factors are listed in Table 9.1.

Table 9.1 Factors associated with a smooth retirement.

- ✓ The retirement is planned.
- ✓ The retirement is voluntary.
- ✓ The athlete has maintained balanced interests.
- ✓ The athlete has achieved personal performance goals.
- ✓ The athlete's environment is supportive.
- ✓ The athlete has completed his or her education.

Based on the factors listed in Table 9.1, the following specific strategies are recommended to ease your personal transition from sport.

Plan for your eventual retirement from sport
One of the most effective strategies for a positive retirement is to simply be prepared for it. Do not wait until your playing days are over before you start preparing for the next phase in your life. Be mindful of the possible areas of retirement stress discussed earlier, and develop a proactive plan that will help you avoid the unpleasant emotions that are often associated with retirement. The recommendations offered in this section will help you identify such a plan.

NOW IS THE TIME TO START PLANNING.

Prepare for future balance in your life
It is healthy and wise to develop and maintain friendships outside the sport setting. Similarly, cultivating other hobbies and interests is important for your overall development. Your sport career is limited in terms of

George Foreman has used his interests outside of boxing to create a financial windfall.

Learn to see yourself as more than just an athlete.

REMEMBER TO FOCUS ON PERFORMANCE AND PROCESS GOALS.

longevity, so you need other interests to fall back on when you retire. This necessitates educational and vocational training, which provides you with an immediate transition to a new career path. Remember, you do not need to sacrifice other interests for the sake of sport. Develop and maintain a healthy balance in your life, and you will have far fewer problems when your competitive career ends.

Develop a "whole person" self-identity

It is very important that you view yourself as a "whole person," not just an athlete. Avoid basing your self-identity solely on sport performance. You won't be competing forever, and performance invariably declines with age. Remember that self-worth is made up of many factors. In addition to being an athlete, you are also a son/daughter, husband/wife, father/mother, sibling, relative, friend, student, and human being. Your self-identity should be formed by a combination of your effectiveness in these and any other roles you assume in life. If you work at developing your conception of self in this manner, when you retire from sport you will experience far less difficulty in terms of personal identity issues. You will also continue to see yourself as a valuable and worthwhile individual once your athletic career is over.

While competing, focus on performance goals, not outcome goals

You can control your performance, but you cannot always control outcomes. For this reason, you should take your satisfaction from your performance and overall improvements in your performance. Focus on task-relevant factors, such as the specific components of a skill or strategy, not on outcomes (wins, losses, points scored, errors). If you use this approach, you will appreciate how it is possible to still feel good about yourself even after a competition loss. Once you leave your sport of choice, the feeling that you have achieved your performance goals will remain indefinitely, making your transition easier.

Seek out social support when you retire

Research indicates that athletes who receive a good deal of positive support from family and friends have an easier time when their playing days are over. Those who have the most difficulty report that they felt alone when their careers ended and would have appreciated more help at that difficult time in their lives. It is therefore important for you to seek out this much-needed support from your family and friends—don't try to do it all alone. It may also prove beneficial to discuss your feelings with other athletes who are going through the same process.

Apply your mental training skills to other aspects of your life

In this book, you learned a variety of mental training skills to help you in your pursuit of sport excellence. You will be happy to hear that these same skills can be successfully applied to other phases of your life, including new interests and pursuits. Positive self-talk, relaxation strategies, imagery, goal setting, attention-control techniques, causal attributions, and strategies for preventing burnout are all effective life skills. For example, the information you learned about building and maintaining confidence can be applied to any new hobby or career you choose to undertake. Confidence will help you perform better in any endeavor. Similarly, if you apply the attention-control strategies to other avenues of your life, you will be able to focus under pressure and perform at your best, regardless of the situation. So remember to use these strategies to your advantage once you have left the sporting environment.

Continuing to exercise is important for health and overall well-being.

Keep exercising

Just because you are retiring from sport does not mean you need to stop moving. At this phase of your life, it is important to keep exercising. Continuing to exercise will not only keep you healthy but will also help you release stress and improve your overall mood. Research indicates that exercise reduces depression, reduces anxiety, improves self-concept, and improves overall mood. This sounds like just the recipe you need to help you adjust to being away from competitive athletics.

View retirement as a time to grow Always try to remember that this transition is actually a time to grow and explore exciting new opportunities. It is not something to be sad about. Think of all the time you normally devote to developing your athletic excellence. Now you will have all that time to spend with your friends and family, to attend school or start a new career, and to follow any other options you choose to pursue. You will also find that you have some time to yourself for a change. So be proactive and continue to seek out exciting new challenges and opportunities. Retirement is a beginning—not an end.

Summary and Conclusions

In this chapter, you learned about the various problems athletes experience when they retire from their sport of choice. You have invested a great deal of time, energy, and commitment during your athletic career. It is only natural to miss it once your playing days are over.

Retirement occurs for a variety of reasons. The most common of these are age, injury, deselection, and free choice. There is a general consensus that the fewest problems occur when the athlete leaves on his or her own terms. But either way, there are several areas of retirement stress. Unless you start to prepare now, you will likely experience feelings of loss in the transition period, because your self-identity and social identity have largely developed from factors associated with being an athlete. You see yourself as an athlete, and you socialize mostly with other athletes. So when your sport career ends, you need to develop a new "picture of yourself." To help you in this process, the chapter recommends several strategies to ease your transition from sport. If you follow these guidelines and realize the goals and action plans you set for yourself in Personal Application 9.2, your retirement from sport will likely be seen as a positive new beginning and not a bad ending.

Personal Application 9.2 What are your personal plans for a successful transition from sport?

Using everything you learned in this chapter, develop three or four personal goals that will prepare you for an easier retirement from your sport. In addition to the goals, outline specifically the action plans you will take to accomplish each goal.

Goal #1: _____

_____

Action plans: _____

_____

_____

Goal #2: _____

_____

Action plans: _____

_____

_____

Goal #3: _____

_____

Action plans: _____

_____

_____

Goal #4: _____

_____

Action plans: _____

_____

_____

THE ATHLETE'S LIBRARY

Grove, J.R., Lavallee, D., Gordon, S., & Harvey, J.H. (1998). Account-making: A model of understanding and resolving distressful reactions to retirement from sport. *The Sport Psychologist, 12,* 52-67.

Kerr, G., & Dacyshyn, A. (2000). The retirement experiences of elite female gymnasts. *Journal of Applied Sport Psychology, 12,* 115-133.

Lavallee, D., Gordon, S., & Grove, J.R. (1997). Retirement from sport and the loss of self-identity. *Journal of Personal and Interpersonal Loss, 2,* 129-147.

Sinclair, D.A., & Orlick, T. (1993). Positive transition from high performance sport. *The Sport Psychologist, 7,* 138-150.

Ungerleiter, S. (1997). Olympic athletes' termination from sport to workplace. *Perceptual and Motor Skills, 84,* 1287-1295.

KEY TERMS

deselection

role restriction

role identity

self-identity

GLOSSARY

anxiety: Mental uneasiness associated with fear and worry.

arousal: The physiological intensity of behavior.

attentional errors: errors that occur as a result of your attentional style.

attentional focus: The ability to focus our attention.

Attentional Style Inventory: A mini version test that measures attentional style.

attributional scheme: The traditional view suggesting basic attributions are categorized into locus of control and stability dimensions.

attributional training: The process of changing your attributions to improve your performance.

autonomic nervous system: That set of organs and glands over which you have little voluntary control.

broad external focus: The ability to "read" a complex environment.

broad internal focus: The ability to comprehend a large amount of information.

burnout: A state of mental, emotional, and physical exhaustion that is associated with your lack of ability to meet the sporting demands.

causal attribution: Your perception of why events happened the way they did.

centering: The ability to center your attention internally, shutting out distracters.

cognitive restructuring: The process of changing our patterns of thought.

cognitive state anxiety: The mental side of state anxiety.

competition plan: Thought-content strategies you use during the actual competition.

coping strategies: Strategies for dealing with uncontrollable events.

cue words: Words that have a specific, emotional, and highly charged meaning to you.

deep breathing: Taking deep breaths when you are feeling stressed out.

deselection: Getting cut from the team.

disruptive away audience: The tendency for a home audience to be nonsupportive or hostile to a visiting team.

distress: Stress that is "bad."

ego-enhancing strategy: The tendency to attribute your successful outcomes to internal factors.

ego-protecting strategy: The tendency to attribute your unsuccessful outcomes to external factors.

emotional reasoning: Assuming your negative feelings reflect the state of reality.

eustress: Stress that is "good."

evaluation component: The more expert the audience, the greater the chances they can improve or hinder your performance.

excessive training: Training time that continues to increase in both time and intensity without any noticeable improvements.

facility familiarity: The tendency for athletes to play better at home because they are more familiar with the playing environment.

5 to 1 count breathing: A combination of deep breathing and self-talk.

focus direction: Internal versus external attentional style.

focus width: Broad versus narrow attentional style.

goal setting: Motivational theory aimed at focusing your efforts and monitoring progress.

home advantage: The finding that many sport teams and athletes perform better at home.

illegal training time: Scheduling practice and training sessions outside the sports legislated guidelines.

inverted-U theory: Performance is improved by increasing arousal up to an optimal point, and then performance deteriorates with further increases in arousal.

labeling: Calling yourself negative names because of an error.

learned helplessness: When you believe events and outcomes are completely beyond your control.

locus of control attributions: Internal versus external perceptions of events.

magnification: The habit of maximizing your interpretation of personal mistakes.

mental filter: The tendency to focus on a single negative detail and to discolor positive ones.

mental rehearsal: The positive visualization of a sport skill or a skill segment.

minimization: The habit of downplaying positive aspects of your performance.

mislabeling: Calling yourself negative names that are emotionally charged or highly colored in language.

mood therapy: How we think determines how we feel.

narrow external focus: The ability to focus on a particular environmental stimulus.

narrow internal focus: The ability to focus your attention inward.

objective goals: Goals that are specifically related to your sport performance.

open-ended measurement: An attribution measurement technique that allows you to classify attributions in your own words.

optimal arousal: The best personal arousal level for your own particular sport.

optimal performance: Doing the best that you can do.

optimism: The tendency to expect the best possible outcome in all situations.

outcome goals: Goals that focus on the final result.

overgeneralization: The tendency to see a single negative event as an endless pattern.

overtraining: A psychophysiological malfunction when you train too hard.

pace of conditioning: The speed of personal conditioning and skill development.

parasympathetic system: The system that selectively reduces the effect of the sympathetic system.

peak performance: When a performance comes together physically and mentally.

perception: What you perceive to be true.

performance goals: Goals that focus on performance improvements.

positive imagery: Seeing a moving picture in your mind's eye "that turns out well."

postcompetition anxiety: The state anxiety that lingers after the actual competition.

precompetition plan: Psychological strategies utilized from the night before competition until the contest begins.

process goals: Goals that deal with specific strategic procedures.

psychological presence: The more spectators are "in your head," the greater the potential for them to hinder your performance.

psychological training: The utilization of psychological interventions to improve sports performance.

role identity: The perceived requirements attached to a social position.

role restriction: The notion that since most athletes associate primarily with other athletes, their ability to assume roles outside of the sport setting is often limited.

self-confidence: The underlying belief in your abilities and attributes.

self-efficacy: The belief that you can successfully perform a task.

self-identity: An athlete's sense of self worth.

self-talk: An internal conversation with yourself.

slump: A specific performance-related phenomenon when you perform at a lower level for a period of time.

social facilitation: The effect of spectators on performance.

social identity: How an athlete "sees" himself or herself in relation to other people.

somatic state anxiety: The physical component of state anxiety.

stability attributions: Stable versus unstable perceptions of events.

staleness: An overall physical and emotional state that is a direct result of your performance drop-off.

state anxiety: A constant feeling of apprehension or worry about an upcoming event.

stress: A nonspecific response of the body to any demand placed on it.

structural rating scale: An attribution measurement technique involving the numerical rating of attributions.

subjective goals: Goals that are unrelated to the actual sport performance.

supportive home audience: The tendency for a home audience to be very supportive and vocal.

sympathetic system: The system involved primarily with bodily symptoms associated with arousal.

thought stopping: Recognizing negative thoughts and developing a "trigger" to change these negative thoughts to positive thoughts.

three-part breathing: A combination of deep breathing and visualization.

training gain: When a positive outcome arises from a training stress.

training stress: The psychophysiological response to increased training.

trait anxiety: A relatively stable predisposition to anxiety.

visualizing: The ability to "see yourself" performing a sport skill

zone: A period of superior functioning, where you perform at a higher level than usual.

REFERENCES

Agnew, G.A., & Carron, A.V. (1994). Crowd effects and the home advantage. *International Journal of Sport Psychology, 25*, 53-62.

Biddle, S.J. (1993). Attribution research and sport psychology. In R. Singer, M. Murphy, & L.K. Tennant (Eds.), *Handbook of research in sport psychology* (pp. 437-464). New York: Macmillan.

Biddle, S.J., & Hill, A.B. (1992). Attributions for objective outcome and subjective appraisal of performance: Their relationships with emotional reactions in sport. *British Journal of Social Psychology, 31*, 215-226.

Bray, S.R. (1999). The home advantage from an individual team performance. *Journal of Applied Sport Psychology, 11*, 116-125.

Burton, D., Weinberg, R., Yukelson, D., & Weigland, D. (1998). The goal effectiveness paradox in sport: Examining the goal practices of collegiate athletes. *The Sport Psychologist, 12*, 404-418.

Cherniss, G. (1995). *Beyond burnout*. London: Routledge.

Coakley, J. (1992). Burnout among adolescents: A personal failure or a social problem? *Social Psychology of Sport Journal, 9*, 271-285.

Cox, R.H. (2002). *Sport psychology: Concepts and applications* (2nd ed.). Dubuque, IA: Brown.

Eklund, R.C. (1996). Preparing to compete: A season long investigation with collegiate wrestlers. *The Sport Psychologist, 10*, 111-131.

Filby, W.C., Maynard, I.W., & Graydon, J.D. (1999). The effect of multiple goal setting strategies on performance outcomes in training and competing. *Journal of Applied Sport Psychology, 11*, 230-246.

Gill, D.L. (1994). A sport and exercise psychology perspective on stress. *Quest, 44*, 20-27.

Gould, D., Medberry, R., Damarjian, N., & Lauer, L. (1999). A survey of mental skills training knowledge, opinions, and practices of junior tennis coaches. *Journal of Applied Sport Psychology, 11*, 28-50.

Gould, D., Udry, E., Tuffey, S., & Loehr, J. (1996). Burnout in competitive junior tennis players: A qualitative psychological assessment. *The Sport Psychologist, 10*, 322-340.

Grove, J.R., Lavallee, D., Gordon, S., & Harvey, J.H. (1998). Account-making: A model of understanding and resolving distressful reactions to retirement from sport. *The Sport Psychologist, 12*, 52-67.

Henschen, K. (1999). Maladaptive fatigue syndrome and emotions in sport. In Y.L. Harris (Ed.), *Emotions in sport* (pp. 231-242). Champaign, IL: Human Kinetics.

Kerr, G., & Dacyshyn, A. (2000). The retirement experiences of elite female gymnasts. *Journal of Applied Sport Psychology*, *12*, 115-133.

Krane, V., Joyce, D., & Rafeld, J. (1994). Competitive anxiety, situation criticality, and softball performance. *The Sport Psychologist*, *8*, 58-72.

Kuipers, H. (1996). How much is too much? Performance aspects of overtraining. *Research Quarterly for Exercise and Sport*, *67*(Suppl. 3), 65-69

Kyllo, L.B., and Landers, D.M. (1995) Goal setting in sport and exercise: A research synthesis to resolve the controversy. *Journal of Sport and Exercise Psychology*, *17*, 117-137.

Landin, D., & Hebert, E.P. (1999). The influence of self-talk on the performance of skilled female tennis players. *Journal of Applied Sport Psychology*, *11*, 263-282.

Lavallee, D., Gordon, S., & Grove, J.R. (1997). Retirement from sport and the loss of self-identity. *Journal of Personal and Interpersonal Loss*, *2*, 129-147.

Madrigal, R., & James, J. (1999). Team quality and the home advantage. *Journal of Sport Behavior*, *22*, 381-398.

Martens, R., Vealey, R.S., & Burton, D. (1990). *Competitive anxiety in sport*. Champaign, IL: Human Kinetics.

Martin, K.A., Moritz, S.E., & Hall, C.R. (1999). Imagery use in sport: A literature review and applied model. *The Sport Psychologist*, *13*, 245-268.

Maynard, I.W., Warwick-Evans, L., & Smith, M.J. (1995). The effects of a cognitive intervention strategy on competitive state anxiety and performance in semiprofessional soccer players. *Journal of Sport and Exercise Psychology*, *17*, 428-446.

Meyers, A.W., Whelan, J.P., & Murphy, S.M. (1998). Cognitive behavioural strategies in athletic performance enhancement. In M. Hersen & A.S. Belack (Eds.), *Handbook of behaviour modification* (pp. 53-65). New York: Plenum Press.

Nideffer, R.M. (1995). *Focus for success*. San Diego, CA: Enhanced Performance Services.

Nideffer, R.M., Sagal, M.S., Lowry, M., & Bond, J. (2000). Identifying and developing world class performers. In *The practice of sport and exercise psychology: International perspectives*. Morgantown, WV: Fitness Information Technology.

Orbach, I., Singer, R., & Murphey, M. (1997). Changing attributions with an attribution training technique related to basketball dribbling. *The Sport Psychologist*, *11*, 294-304.

Orbach, I., Singer, R., & Price, S. (1999). An attribution training program and achievement in sport. *The Sport Psychologist*, *13*, 69-82.

Rotella, R. (1996). *Golf is a game of confidence*. New York: Simon and Schuster.

Schunk, D.H. (1995). Self-efficacy, motivation and performance. *Journal of Applied Sport Psychology*, *7*, 112-137.

Sinclair, D.A., & Orlick, T. (1993). Positive transition from high performance sport. *The Sport Psychologist*, *7*, 138-150.

Ungerleiter, S. (1997). Olympic athletes' termination from sport to workplace. *Perceptual and Motor Skills*, *84*, 1287-1295.

Williams, J.M. (2001). *Applied sport psychology: Personal growth to peak performance* (4th ed.). Mountain View, CA: Mayfield.

Wright, E.F., Voyer, D., Wright, R.D. & Roney, C. (1995). Supporting audiences and performance under pressure: The home-ice disadvantage in hockey championships. *Journal of Sport Behavior, 18*, 21-28.

Ziegler, S.G. (1994). The effects of attentional shift training on the execution of soccer skills: A preliminary investigation. *Journal of Applied Behavioral Analysis, 27*, 55-552.

INDEX

PHOTO CREDITS

Photos were reproduced with permission from the Faculty of Physical Education and Health, University of Toronto

Additional photography provided by Corbis/Magma Photo, Niko Slana, PhotoDisc, Sport Books Publisher, Sports Illustrated, York University.

Every effort has been made to acknowledge correctly and contact the source and/or copyright holder of each picture, and Sport Books Publisher apologizes for any unintentional errors or omissions, which will be corrected in future editions of this book.

	Pages
Corbis/Magma Photo Inc.	70
Niko Slana	19, 96, 167
PhotoDisc	front cover, 15, 80, 90 (basketball), 92, 99, 137, 146, 166, 177, 189
Sport Books Publisher	30, 31, 33, 103, 123, 164, 179
Sports Illustrated	18, 46, 135, 156, 173
University of Toronto	inside front cover, 7, 10, 14, 16, 17, 22, 24, 26, 32, 44, 50, 53, 56, 60, 61, 62, 64, 68, 71, 79, 87, 100, 104, 105 (basketball, football), 116, 118, 124, 129, 136, 148, 171, 176, 184, inside back cover
York University	95